AFTER A WHILE YOU JUST GET USED TO IT

AFTER A WHILE YOU JUST GET USED TO IT

A Tale of Family Clutter

GWENDOLYN KNAPP

GOTHAM BOOKS

GOTHAM BOOKS
An imprint of Penguin Random House
375 Hudson Street
New York, New York 10014

Copyright © 2015 by Gwendolyn Knapp
LIBRARY OF CONGRESS CATALOGING-IN-PUBLICATION DATA
has been applied for.

ISBN 978-1-592-40913-6

Printed in the United States of America
10 9 8 7 6 5 4 3 2 1

Set in Palatino LT STD   Designed by Elke Sigal

In loving memory of Sue and Susie.
And for Mom. I love you. Don't kill me.

Contents

I.
Holiday Greetings

II.
Nut Treasures

III.
Adult-Sized Caboodles

Prologue: Family Clutter

There had been others, in the early days after Mom's divorce, men who looked like Magnum, P.I., and carted us around in their midlife-crisis-mobiles. This was back when most guys liked to wear the least amount of shorts possible to show off the greatest amount of body hair possible: the mid-1980s. I'd witnessed the worst of it from the backseat of cars driven by dudes who never stuck around. Dating, I'd learned by the time I was nine, was full of embarrassment and letdown. Not for kids, but for the single parent. Mainly, I'd learned, it was a means to see who would stick around after Mom started yelling. By the time she was in her second year of architecture school in Tampa, two months deep into the fall semester, she'd found a new victim.

Molly and I knew right away. We found Mom in the bathroom one Saturday acting all nutsy: applying a home perm, trying on a new shade of rouge, and singing Linda Ronstadt into the mirror at the top of her lungs, locking us out, though I was about to soil my pants.

"I can't hold it any longer," I told her.

"Well, that's nothing new," she said, waltzing out with her silk kimono draped over her thin shoulders.

"What's wrong with you?" Molly asked Mom, but we already knew. Soon she would have her good pair of suede boots on, pretending she didn't count screaming as a hobby.

"Nothing." She smiled. "Can't I just be happy if I feel like it?"

On Saturdays, she usually liked to wallow in bed until noon, warning us to keep it down with our WCW impersonations and suffocation-by-pillow competition. Then she'd rise like the dead in her frilly cotton nightgown, downing a pot of black-tar coffee and slumping over her drafting table for hours. We thought that was her happy.

"I've met someone," she told us, buffing her nails, sharpening them perhaps, a deranged twinkle in her eye.

"You should go lie back down," I insisted.

"Yeah," Molly said. "You got a new Spiegel catalog in the mail."

That was the spirit. A healthy dose of perfect models in clothes you couldn't afford was a sure way to bring any single mother back to her normal state, but Mom wasn't having it.

"His name is John," she continued. She said this as if *John* were the most exotic name ever spoken.

"John," I said, and yawned. I couldn't help it. If pronounced in German, *John* basically was *yawn*.

Prologue: Family Clutter

When John swung into our side yard that evening at fifty miles an hour, screeching to a halt next to our rusted wagon, it was no surprise Mom still wasn't ready to go. My mother ran late for everything, always had. There never was a chorus recital, movie, living Christmas tree, or Easter pageant we'd ever seen the first thirty minutes of. The story of Jesus, for me, had always begun with the wino years. Some people blame repeated tardiness on selfishness and just plain being rude, but there were things working against Mom. She had a hard time getting out of bed due to the stresses of life—no child support, two nagging daughters, graduate school, an ailing father.

My sister and I sat on the back steps and watched as John emerged from the ugliest car I'd ever seen, uglier than our own even, a turd-boat on wheels with one ill-fitting, sickly green driver's-side door. It opened with several loud pops, like bones being ripped from their sockets.

John was a good-looking guy with a head of dirty-blond hair and an overgrown mustache, wearing aviators and denim on denim, smiling at us with perfect white teeth. He wasn't perfect though. He was from Ohio. Land of corn and white bread. We were from here, Florida, land of lightning and mangrove swamps, and could detect interlopers as easy as red ants in the sugar sand.

"Nice car," my sister said under her breath as we watched John try to slam the green door shut three times. He leaned all his weight against it and gave it a big bump with his hip like I'd seen some fat, drunk bridesmaids do to each other at a cousin's wedding over the summer, knocking the baby's breath out of each other's hair during "Disco Duck."

"Thing's broke," John said, instead of introducing himself. "I had these guys at a body shop fix it and they screwed me over. Story of my life."

He spoke to us like we were his drinking buddies, at nine and twelve years old. He took one look at our skeletal plum trees, our inflatable kiddie pool folded in on itself like a yard omelet, and said, "Sure is a nice place you got here."

"Isn't it?" we said, showing off the tarp-covered junk and a pile of wood where a playhouse used to be before the neighbor kids burned it down.

"No, it's really nice. It's real old Florida," he said, and smiled.

I'd heard that before. *Real old Florida* meant overgrown and mysterious. It meant unpaved and unlike the rest of Holiday, Florida, with its strip malls and developments. It meant cow patties, and rotten oranges, and septic tanks that occasionally flooded the yard. It meant oak trees draped in shawls of moss as if they transformed into elderly women at the stroke of midnight.

Usually when people came over, their eyes bulged in fear of the house, wrapped in vines and giant spiderwebs. John walked around with his eyes bulging in wonder, claiming, "They don't make beauties like this nowadays." Rubbing his hands on the siding and concluding, "Why, I bet that's lead paint."

"Taste it and tell us," Molly said.

It was obvious Mom and John already had one thing in common: the ability to stand and stare at a building long enough to drive any normal person insane. Mom had been hauling us across the state every weekend for a year to visit private universities, skyscrapers, and other so-called structures of architectural merit that she wanted to study and sketch. Where I saw various buildings with no public restrooms or trees and hard benches that hurt my tailbone while I writhed around with boredom, she enthusiastically commended concrete slabs for their clean lines and postmodernism. For studying so many aspects of architectural design, she certainly didn't apply them to our own house, besides creating new walls out of stacks of baskets and magazines. When we moved into Aunt Ruby's old cracker house three years before, we never moved any of her things out. We just stacked our things on top as if preserving some avant historical movement: "Southern hoarder trapped in haunted house" chic.

"Enter," we said to John.

Mom, of course, wasn't done in the bathroom. Give that woman a day, and she could spend it scrutinizing every hair, pore, and new development with her body. Give her a date, and she'd need to be locked in there overnight.

"Your date is here," Molly screamed.

"Yeah," I said. "*Your date* is here."

"Just a second," she said.

We showed John our ancient piano that poured out dust like a steam engine when you played chopsticks too fast, our sewing machine underneath mounds of fabric, our bookshelves and the bookshelves behind them. Aunt Ruby hadn't lived here in a while, not after she kept wandering into the woods and the men in our family had to come out and capture her like she was a wild animal. Found her sitting on a stump in the forest, asking them if they'd come by for iced tea. *No, ma'am*, they said, *we come to take you to Anclote Manor*. But all her things were preserved under our own. Coming from a place like Palm Beach, where we'd lived with enough space for our things in a sixties-style ranch house until our parents split up in 1986, was not only culture shock for Molly and me but also an electric shock if you attempted to plug certain lamps into certain sockets.

"Look at these Caboodles," we instructed John, but he paid no mind.

"Why, get a load of these window moldings."

He had us cornered in the living room, lecturing us on the difference between craftsman and shotgun houses, when Mom emerged from the bathroom, resplendent and dewy. She could turn it on when she wanted to; she had the ability to become somebody different with makeup and an outfit alone. She was so beautiful then, so fluffy haired, so stinking with the toxic combination of Elizabeth Arden Red Door and perm chemicals that I could no longer detect the smell of the decaying animal in the wall or the years of fried-chicken grease emitted by the kitchen, where the wallpaper had begun to unpeel itself in rebellion.

"Is the perfume too much?" Mom asked. "I can't tell."

"No, it's great," John said, a clear indication he had indeed tasted the paint.

I applied my Dr Pepper lip gloss and pulled on my deflated Nike Airs, watching Mom give John a hug before saying her world-famous line, "Well, excuse our junk."

Certainly if you went back in time and researched our

family crest, it would read *Lord, bless this mess.* But John didn't mind our junk. He felt comfortable with it, excited even.

"You have a lot of cool stuff," he said. "This place is great."

She smiled, and I knew it was over then. We'd be stuck with these two loonies forever, listening to them talk about the joys of accordion doors and carpet samples. Molly sulked and wrapped herself up in a baggy sweater, loathing her existence like every middle-school student who'd ever been forced to come out of their bedroom. By *bedroom* I mean the square foot of living space she had carved out in the front junk room.

"Well, where are we going?" I asked. At least we usually got a free meal out of the deal.

"We?" Mom laughed. "Oh, no, honey. You're getting dropped off at Grandma and Grandpa's. John and I are going dancing."

John didn't know that getting involved with our family was a lot like getting initiated into a street gang. You might get kicked in the forehead, pistol-whipped, or sliced with a box cutter, sure, but most definitely you'd pierce an extremity with a fishhook, dislocate your shoulder with the recoil of a shotgun, or jump off a bridge into shallow water while drunk and then have to wear a cage around your head for a year because you broke your neck something terrible.

By the time we pulled into Grandma's driveway, Mom's face looked a tad concerned about it all. My sister and I stared at the back of John's head, which was in no way bald. The stresses of life had not yet started eating away at his scalp the way it had all the previous men, including my father, whose own hair had eventually fled like a dandelion in the wind.

"Daddy hasn't been feeling too well after his accident," Mom told John before we got out of the car. She was more beautiful than I'd ever seen, could've told him to floor it to Acapulco and he would've obeyed. Any man would have. "I don't know if you want to come in or just wait out here. It's up to you."

This is the same thing that my phys-ed coach told the flabby kids who passed out during the running portion of the annual Physical Fitness Test each September in the glaring sun. Coach called this the moment you could be either a chump or a champ, as if heatstroke had never killed a person.

"Let's go," John said.

Then Grandma was beaming in her pink sweat suit and apron, hugging John in the doorway. "It's so nice to meet you. Welcome. I'm just making some chicken and dumplings for the girls."

She gave us hugs. Then she screamed past the wall of Grandpa's collector's plates and toward the living room, "Sam, they're here."

This happened to be around the time my grandpa had been struck by lightning for the second time in his life, so nobody really knew what was going on in his head. When electricity fries you from the inside out like a microwave does a hot dog, it makes mysterious things happen. His hair had gone stark white in recent days and he wore gauze over his shoulder, where a black sore oozed like stigmata. He'd mostly taken to communicating via dirty looks and grunts alone. A simple *hey* might mean *Oh, look, a new* Matlock *episode,* while an *eh* might mean *If you kids don't stop talking through this* Matlock *episode, I'm going to fart you out of the goddamn room.* Thunder continued to roll long after Grandpa's lightning strike.

I'd learned in our annual pre-Thanksgiving Native American studies that the word *Ohio* signified "great river," and now I could detect one running from John's hairline to his armpits, where two great lakes were forming.

"Daddy," Mom said. "This is John."

"Hey," Grandpa said, apathetic as a Soviet ice-skating judge. Always had been. Even when my parents split up, Grandpa raised not a brow in surprise, not that he had any left after the first time lightning singed them off his face like caterpillars from a tree. Grandpa had also survived a bleeding ulcer in '86 and a bypass surgery in '88, so nothing much impressed him. If you needed a reminder of his life motto, it was kept above the toilet in the guest bathroom: a framed poster of a train pitching off a bridge into a river with the words SHIT HAPPENS scrawled across the top.

He looked right through Mom and John toward the television, where Andy Rooney was griping about something or another. The clock ticked away as if counting every single moment of one's wasted time.

"It's nice to meet you, sir," John said as he and Mom took a seat on the couch.

"Eh," Grandpa said. We turned our attention to the television, which was neatly stacked on a larger, archaic television that no longer worked. It was all very pleasant. The television of my day, stacked upon the television of my mom's day. A large smile even snaked across Grandpa's face as he vaporized the room. Silent but deadly.

※

If, as Maya Angelou once claimed, love is indeed like a virus, then Mom and John clearly needed medication. That fall, the days stretched out long and sweet as the saltwater taffy sold near the livestock tent at the county fair. Sweetness amid the cow patties.

"Let's go," Mom told us one Saturday morning, rising earlier than I'd ever witnessed.

"Where?" I asked, certain we'd be carted off to see arts and craftsmanship in Hyde Park, or an old plantation up in Micanopy, which, even worse, had antique malls all along the way.

"To John's apartment. They have canoes you can rent at his complex. Doesn't that sound nice?"

"You're joking, right?" Molly said, poking her head from her pain cave, from which a wall of darkness and *Master of Puppets* emanated.

John's apartment was nothing nice, no artwork or books, just golf clubs and a guitar case, an old television that when turned on exploded from the inside as if badly poisoned, and a dining table covered in architecture plans.

"Could use a little perking up," Mom told us. "But not bad, huh?"

"Sure," we said, sitting on his itchy brown plaid sofa, direct from the leisure-suit era.

We rented a canoe from a man in the office and hauled it out to the Hillsborough River. The day was chilly, a cold front having whipped through town overnight, and it became evident two hours in that we were not at all dressed properly.

"Row harder," Mom urged me and Molly, both of us freezing in long-sleeved shirts and jeans. "It'll warm you up."

At first it did, and it was fun. We saw otters and a gator. Then Mom started chanting *hi yai yai yai* like a Native American because she claimed it helped her row better. She could row and row. She could've rowed for days. She could've rowed until we ran out of river. She didn't want to turn around even after we'd been aboard for three hours without eating.

"Excuse me, Sacagawea," Molly complained. "But it's way past lunch."

"You're telling me," John said. "I'm starving."

"Well, there's a Shoney's upriver a bit," Mom said. People on long expeditions were always claiming such things before they wound up trapped in a cave somewhere, eating a shoelace or a loved one's entrails. "We can stop there and eat. I don't think I have cash though."

"I've got cash," John said. "I took some out yesterday."

We paddled hard for another hour, finally reaching the Shoney's, the sun now sinking lower into the sky. We were shivering and tired. We hauled the canoe onto the trash-strewn shore and climbed the hill to the parking lot and toward the warm glow of the buffet heat lamps. We sat down in a comfortable vinyl booth and thawed out. I was pointing out the club sandwich and hot chocolate on the menu when a look of horror swept over John's face.

"My wallet," he said, checking his pockets and jean jacket. "I can't find my wallet."

"How y'all doing this afternoon?" our waitress asked. Her brown polyester uniform clung tightly to her skin, and a shiny name tag assured us her name was Tish.

"Oh. Okay," Mom said politely. "John here may have lost his wallet though."

"Oh," Tish said. "You didn't drop it on the floor, did you?"

Suddenly an embarrassing fuss ensued, and Molly sunk down in the booth, blushing or maybe just third-degree sunburned. Tish searched all over, interrupting diners to check under tables. John went back out across the parking lot and to the canoe, coming back a few minutes later, distraught.

"I don't know where it is," he said, and Mom's face twisted a little.

My stomach writhed. The table next to us cast looks of pity upon our starving party, our chapped lips, our hands bleeding from the day's hard labor of rowing. A large steaming cauldron of apple cobbler arrived on their table, ice cream melting over the top, and they all made orgasmic noises like everyone did in the early days after that annoying tuna-sandwich scene from *When Harry Met Sally*.

"Oh my god," Molly said. "I want that cobbler."

"I would kill for that cobbler," I said.

"I would drown you in a swimming pool for that cobbler."

"I would come back to life and drown you in a swimming pool and eat the cobbler on top of your dead bloated body."

"You two stop it now," Mom said, reaching for her purse. "I might have enough for one cobbler."

She had no cash in there though. We already knew what she was reaching for: the five hundred pennies she kept in a sticky old pouch, which was heavy enough to use as a weapon if anybody ever tried to mug her. She could hold it out and say, *Please, mister, this is all I have,* before clobbering him in the pie hole.

Tish winced as we left stacks of change all over the table for her. She was still loading coins into her apron when we got back in the canoe and headed downriver, bits of trash floating alongside of us.

"Oh," John exclaimed when we made it back to his apartment that night, streams of snot frozen to our shirts like suspenders. "Looks like I left my wallet on the dining table."

Not everything stays sweet forever. That winter, as the muted sun began to take its early afternoon dip, my sister and I watched as a handful of cousins and Mom's brother, Jack, met in the back field, come to take Grandpa's hunting dogs away. They loaded them in crates and set them in the back of several trucks, hauling them off the property and over to Moon Lake, where somebody could take care of them.

Then one day Grandma picked me up from latchkey like usual, Molly already riding shotgun with her clarinet case, fresh from jazz band practice. She drove us back to the house. Say this day was like the rest. I might tell you how the peacocks, having wandered over from the tree farm, shrieked in the front yard as Grandma pulled in the driveway. How people at the strip mall convenience store across the street stood around in their jean jackets like they always did, cursing into pay phones and smoking cigarettes, their backs against the glass of a video rental store as if stuck to flypaper. But this day was not like the rest.

We barged into the house. I threw down my book bag and ran to the guest bathroom to go pee, and there I walked in on Grandpa, who was seated on the toilet.

"Sorry," I said, but he didn't even look. I shut the door and ran back to the kitchen down the hall.

"Look here at this," Grandma said, showing me a squirrel tail their hunting buddy Deon had dropped off.

"We could make a hat like Davy Crockett," I said, holding it up to my head.

"That was a coonskin cap, dork," Molly said.

"So?"

Molly held out a porcelain bird with an actual chip on its shoulder for me to see, another new knickknack Grandma had found at Goodwill. She loved to collect little porcelain birds. She poured me a bowl of Grape-Nuts doused in sugar and heavy cream, the way I always took it.

"There's ants in the Grape-Nuts again," I told her.

"Protein," she said.

When the bathroom door opened, I swung around and hopped up from my bar stool. There stood Grandpa in front of the bathroom, down the hall. He went to take a step and clutched both walls with his giant hands. He stared at me, and I stared back, both of us frozen.

"Grandma," I said. "I think something is wrong with Grandpa."

Then it was happening; something *was* wrong. Grandpa's

14

eyes rolled up in his head, his knees buckled, and he collapsed to the floor.

"Sam?" Grandma called.

She ran to him, knelt down beside him, repeating his name. *Sam*, she kept saying, *Sam*. Even after they'd gone out to the stilt house, a mile out in the gulf—you could only get there by boat—to fish, and he'd lain down on a metal cot to rest and lightning struck, singeing the carpet and setting the kitchen ablaze, she'd managed to get him back into shore through the storm while my great-aunt Jane and uncle Jim stayed to put out the fire. Now she lifted his arm and placed it on his belly but it slid down and landed on the floor, and we knew there was nothing she could do.

"Stay in the kitchen," she yelled as we came close. She'd never yelled at us like that before, and she never would again. "Call Uncle Jack. Call an ambulance."

My sister and I obeyed. We called Uncle Jack, Grandpa's spitting image, who lived right next door. He didn't even hang up the phone, just came running across the yard, all three hundred pounds of him. Then I stood in the doorway, watching them, as Molly talked to the emergency operator.

When the ambulance came, we were left alone in the living room, my sister and me, neither of us saying much of anything, just looking at our own reflections in the window of the big empty living room. My cousins got ahold of Mom at the architecture school, and she booked it back to the hospital. Came back with Grandma, Uncle Jack, and Aunt Susie hours later, all of them with bloodshot eyes.

"He's gone," Mom cried on the ride back to the house. "I can't believe it. I just don't know what we'll do, what Mommy will do."

One thing Grandma had no interest in doing: giving away Grandpa's guns, *National Geographics*, or collector's plates, because she, like everyone else in the family, was a genuine pack rat. When an old relative dies, pack rats usually take in all they can from the person's home as if they're adopting abandoned children. It's their duty. Since Grandma kept all his things, her kids had to find new ways to fill their void. Pack rats build up the world around them, separating themselves with a cloak of comfort from the outside world, which is probably why, after a few months, Mom decided that it would be best if John moved in with us at Aunt Ruby's.

For most people dating in the modern age—the year 1991!— first came love, then came marriage, then came babies in the baby carriage. For Mom and John, first came love. Then came the marriage of the world's ugliest automobiles. Then came the scabies. Lord knows who brought it home, but it spread all over Aunt Ruby's house, infesting the green carpet, the white lace curtains, and the *Star Wars* sheets on my bunk bed. Mom was ashamed and cried. Molly laughed to her friends on the phone and said, *I knew we were white trash,* then listened to R.E.M. and cried. John went to the driving range, and I just itched. I scratched at scabies with my fingers, with my Barbies, with my hairbrush behind my knees. The walls of the house weren't rough enough for my back. I thought about heating the curling iron and burning out my armpits.

Not even this girl, let's call her Carol Show, who rode my bus and played French horn with me in band knew I had scabies, because I donned more turtlenecks than an English teacher. At least my scabies went away. We washed everything in the house and stayed with Grandma. Carol Show got scabies in seventh grade and they lasted a whole year. I wasn't her friend. One day she told me, *You've turned into such a good horn player.* She said this to sit next to me on the bus. She wanted me to give her compliments, but I didn't. She wore halter tops and high-heeled sandals.

When the bus drove past the house on Dixie Highway, because we looped past it twice before I got dropped off, naturally, Carol Show said, "That's your house?"

She knew it was. Just like I knew she didn't live in a house at all.

"That's cool you guys have a fireplace," she said.

"What?"

"Isn't that a chimney coming out the roof?"

"Oh, yeah. We got a nice fireplace," I lied. That chimney was really some vent for the old brown kerosene heater that we never used except for stacking phone books on. If we used it, Mom swore, we'd burn the house down, so when it got cold we'd turn on several long brown space heaters from Aunt Ruby's collection and stand in front of them. The metal coils burned the hair off your legs if you stood too close.

"That's cool," Carol Show said, and smiled. It wasn't comfortable to sit in a seat with two French horns and a girl who smelled like body odor, the type that doesn't belong to an eleven-year-old girl, the type that rubs off on you only if cheap men hug on you all the time.

"It's pretty useless," I said. "It doesn't get cold enough to use the fireplace, you know."

"Do you ever climb up inside it? I've heard about climbing up in one."

"No," I said, "there's bats in there."

"Bats?"

"Yes. A lot of bats," I said as she scratched at her arm. I'd heard bats in my grandma's chimney, before she smoked them out into the daylight and they showered the sky like flapping tar.

I didn't say anything about Carol Show's scabies. I didn't say, *Once I had scabies too, girl.* Her scabies may have lasted longer than a year, but she stopped catching the bus and stopped going to school. She lived in the trailer park behind the Checkers where Molly later worked. Every day she got off the bus and lugged her French horn case down the highway toward home, strutting like a teen prostitute with a half-melted suitcase. Then one day she just disappeared. Maybe she went somewhere. Maybe she carried that horn to Vegas or New York or Tijuana. Maybe she carried that horn until her arm felt numb, and it must have been the best feeling. Do you know how that is, to not be itchy anymore?

One day during the next fall, 1992, after it had rained and rained for months, Mom decided we needed to get out of the house for a bit, take a ride over to Anclote Beach to get our toes in the sand and chase some hermit crabs. She needed to clear her head since some cousins had stopped by and told her that Aunt Ruby wasn't doing too well. They were going to sell the house when she died. Our rent-free days were numbered. To make matters worse, a declawed house cat had shown up in our yard after getting hit by a car, and John had maxed out his credit cards on emergency surgery, vet fees, and a crate big enough for a kidnapped child to live in. "We need to be saving money to move," Mom scolded him. "Not spending it on a cat that isn't even ours." But soon enough Sheldon was ours, wearing a plastic cone of shame around his neck, so he fit in with the thirty other lampshades in the house. Mom treated him like she would any new member of the family that constantly cried and peed on her good towels: with utter disdain.

John drove us down the winding roads that wrapped through saw grass and stubby knees of mangroves that lurked in shallow muck. He was rambling about one thing or another, not paying attention to the road.

"This is it!" we screamed. "This is the turn!"

He swung in at thirty miles an hour, and I watched the faces of four terrified passengers in a brand-new Ford Taurus. They were trying to exit the park and we plowed our metallic turd right into them. The hood of their car curled up and away like the silver part of a scratch-off ticket after you take a quarter to it. My mother screamed at the top of her lungs.

"We've had an accident," I said.

"Thank god you had your seat belts on," Mom said.

"Too bad," Molly said, rolling her eyes. "If only my brains had been bashed in."

"That's not funny."

Mom was angrier than I'd seen her in a while. "Just what the hell were you thinking?" she asked John. "I mean, god-damn it. Who drives like that, you fucking asshole?"

"I was trying to make the turn, Margie. I'm sorry."

The people in the other car were getting out now, upset and shaking their heads. The driver opened his door and stared at the wreckage, holding his head with both hands as if it might come off if he didn't. Other cars were starting to accumulate, wanting to turn in or out of the park, and we were blocking them.

"Call the cops," the driver urged a lady in his car.

"I'm really sorry, man," John said, getting out. "I don't know what I was thinking."

"You weren't thinking," Mom sniped under her breath. "Duh."

We stayed in the car for a while and finally Mom agreed we could walk over to the playground.

"Are you believing that?" she said. "What an asshole."

"It was an accident," Molly said. "That's why it's called an accident."

This didn't please my mother. She was in some sort of mood now. "Just go play while we deal with this. Okay?"

That sounded good to us. Mainly we just sat on a picnic table watching the cop roll up and the tow trucks arrive. We chased hermit crabs on the beach and then wandered over to the old Indian mounds near the edge of the park. You could still find arrowheads the Calusa had left there if you looked hard enough. We'd been told our great-great-great-grandfather had cured their chief's daughter of an illness with some medicine and received twenty-two acres of coastal land for doing so back in the early 1800s, but that was probably all a lie. He'd likely just gotten the land because he was a surveyor, and none of it belonged to us anymore, so what did it matter? I looked out to the water, where the sun was setting on the old pilings men built to collect bird shit for fertilizer, and beyond them were the stilt houses a mile out in the water, out where my grandfather had been struck by lightning. By next year, the "No Name Storm" would obliterate most of the shacks, including my family's, and the state would not let them rebuild. But now they looked like something sacred, a colony on the horizon, a place I'd rather be.

"Where do you think we're going to move?" I asked my sister.

"Does it matter?" she said. "This whole place is a dump."

Grandma came to our rescue when the cops were done.

"The guy wound up being from Ohio," John told her on the ride back. She tried to drown him out with Billy Ray Cyrus on the radio.

"Turns out he's from a city not even fifteen minutes from where I grew up," John yelled. "What are the chances?"

"Well, you still have to deal with his insurance," Mom scolded him. "So don't go thinking he's a saint."

She rode in the backseat with us, and I leaned into her, letting her hug me tight, hoping it might perk her up a bit. She looked pretty even though she was angry, her perm starting to frizz a little. I stared at the back of John's head, his hair as thick as the day I'd first seen him. He was all amped up, singing along to Billy Ray. He stuck his head out the window and hooted for no reason, smiling at the passing grid of ugly house upon ugly house and the miles of saw grass beyond them.

"Oh, give it a rest," Mom barked, and John sat back, slicking his hair, only a tiny piece out of place, the rest seemingly unperturbed. That was the year of "Achy Breaky Heart."

I.

Holiday Greetings

Southern Gothic

F ast food usually turns people into lard butts, but back in high school, it turned Molly into a goth. It was the Checkers that did it, the one on US 19 in Holiday, where life was never a holiday but a halfway point between mermaids and Scientologists. I don't know why all the goths worked at Checkers. Maybe because of the uniform, corporate Dracula: black pants, black shirt, ketchup stains like dried blood. Checkers had concrete picnic tables stabbed through the heart by umbrellas that teetered the wrong way in the mildest wind. Skeletal trees withered away in large stone planters, unable to penetrate the cement underneath them—there was no room for them to grow, to flourish, and they all slowly died. Most kids in town knew the feeling.

Before Checkers, Molly was like most teenage redheads in 1995, a virginal band nerd with bad self-esteem and oversized Cobain cardigans for days. She'd already secured a near-perfect SAT score and a National Merit Scholarship to the university of her choice, which guaranteed she'd ditch town in a few months. What she didn't have was a car, the actual, physical means of getting out.

Mom's car wasn't the type of thing she could pass on to Molly for college. It barely made it to Tampa and back each day, terrifying most people when she merged onto the highway the way a hippo might when it explodes from the dark waters of the Nile. It often refused to start, usually when we went to the grocery store, so we could sit in the roasting sun with our ice cream melting, milk curdling, heads of lettuce turning to fine silk. Whole hours we sat there as she'd turn the key to elicit a grinding sound like tectonic plates, as the lining drooped from the ceiling and rested on our heads. Pimply cart collectors stared as bits of white foam lining snowed from the windows.

"If those idiots can work here," Molly asked, "why can't I?"

"Why are you so concerned with what all the other idiots are doing?" Mom asked.

"Because I want a job and a car."

"What do you need a car for?" Mom asked, pumping the gas and flooding the engine.

"So I can drive off a cliff."

Besides the humiliation accumulation from riding around with Mom, as well as an interminable resentment from a life of indentured servitude at the house on Missouri Avenue (John had just bought it a year before: a sky-blue testament to the 1960s. Cement block, the type people attach to their ankles when they really want to drown.), there were signs my sister might turn goth, proof of some sinister affectation. She had pale skin that didn't get darker in the sun unless all her freckles converged in pigmented splotches. She always had her face in a depressing book, Dostoevsky or Kafka, half of which were spotted in blood because her nose had bled like a coke whore's since the day she was born.

Everybody knows goths love blood, almost as much as they love the free coffee refills at Denny's, but we just didn't see it coming.

She started senior year as a normal, cynical nerd. Drum major, toting around a sordid history with the band orgy—a group of kids who'd spent years perfecting the fine art of blowing. Their zitty dating circle involved a lot of backstabbing, youth group, and Shoney's breakfast buffet, but Molly was never as Vanilla Fields as the rest of them. Halfway through the semester, her only tie to them was Kelly Bell, a pious flautist with hair down to her butt, who drove us to school every morning because she lived nearby. Molly was transforming day by day, nearing eighteen, blasting Morrissey, switching out her Esprit sweater vests for black tank tops and JNCOs and usually ending conversations with Mom in suicide threats or passive-aggressive nothings. *I'd rather slit my wrists than eat your beef Stroganoff again. Not that you'd care.*

Maybe Mom did care, but nothing says *Go on and leave for college already* quite like banishing somebody to a patio. That's where my sister lived—in the "Florida room"—along with

Mom's sewing machine, drafting table, blueprints, and hundreds of patterns and boxes of fabric. It was air-conditioned at least. The entire room was windows, should've been the sunniest room in the house, but Molly kept the shades drawn dark, so as not to let her communist Russian artwork fade. She'd always gotten the shaft on bedrooms—had pretty much lived in a glorified storage closet at our old house—but then again, she was leaving in less than a year. She closed herself in there every afternoon, mourning our impecunious fate, studying flash cards, sorting through her acceptance letters to premed programs, unaware that she'd been destined to become a librarian since the first time she cataloged her *Baby-Sitters Clubs* and *Sassy* magazines by publication date alone. Maybe she felt isolated, deprived, depraved: Her room *was* separated from the rest of the house by a rickety sliding glass door that revealed her anchoritic life like an aquarium.

"Bubbles?" I asked her, my nostrils pressed to the glass. "What are you doing in there?" It was the era of Michael Jackson and Lisa Marie, and my next-door neighbor Andrea and I had been known to speak solely in falsetto.

"Nothing," Molly said. "Go away."

Every day after JV soccer practice, Andrea and I came back to the house on Missouri Avenue to practice salsa to a Gloria Estefan CD and watch MTV while eating our microwaved nachos. Later in the evening, we'd flee to her house next door while Mom came home and fought with Molly. We wore our shin guards, our green knee-high socks, and sandals. From the waist up we looked like freshmen, waist down like Ninja Turtles.

"Hey, Wendy," Andrea said. "Come here."

She was on the toilet, her green Umbros pulled down. She always took dumps with the door open no matter whose house she was at. She never wasted a moment of her time being silent, born to talk even midturd or half naked before school while blow-drying her hair.

"I think I'm in love," she said.

"With who?"

"Justin Case."

It's probably not the best idea to fall in love with the tail end of a precautionary measure, but it could've been worse. There was an actual kid at our school named Rusty Nails and another who went by Long Dang.

"But he's dating some ho," she said, wiping herself.

She flushed it all away, and Gloria Estefan was turned up, our sandals replaced with high heels. Our dance moves spilled across the terrazzo in the living room, where the walls still featured pink and purple sponge paint with fake gold trim around the center like a shiny belt, as if the previous owner thought the place needed to be dressed in a Jazzercise outfit. We never dreamed of painting over it. We just piled all our junk inside and danced around it.

Inside the Florida room my sister ignored us, studying, reading, listening to her headphones. We turned down the music and tapped on the glass. The caged animal in its natural habitat will search for a hiding spot among cluttered furniture when being studied, even giving up the need for food and water.

"Bubbles, this is Lisa Marie. We made nachos for you, baby."

"Come eat your nachos, Bubbles."

She was up to something in there, talking on the cordless telephone to somebody, waving us off. Ten minutes into *Singled Out*, she finally emerged. She had enjoyed a Coke and a single nacho, the layer of American cheese now cooled to plastic solids, when her nose started bleeding. She sprawled across the couch, and I got a spoon from the freezer—she always kept one in there for her nosebleeds. She pressed it against the back of her neck and I got her a washcloth for the blood.

"Poor Bubbles," I said. I moonwalked across the terrazzo to the sliding glass door, and because she was incapacitated, I crossed the threshold to her room, examining the papers on her bed.

"Oh, you're gonna get in trouble," I said. "What is this?"

"An application for Checkers, you asshole." Then she made an unnatural snorting sound, the one she always made when swallowing large amounts of her own blood.

Most parents would probably want their children to get a job in high school and experience a taste of the real world, but not Mom. A lifelong graduate student, she'd always been adamantly against working.

"Checkers?" she inquired over beef stew. "What are you, nuts?"

"You're being a little rash, don't you think?" John asked Mom, but there was nothing little about her rash. It traveled up her neck to her face when she was constantly pushed to address a subject she didn't want to talk about.

"I need a car," Molly said. She repeated this over cube steaks and pork chops, over poor-boy potatoes and tacos, until our dinners unfurled like a kindergartner's spelling bee.

"No," Mom said. "N-O."

By the time we reached our weekly beef Stroganoff, Molly had the sliding glass door locked and refused to join the table. Mom and her faced off betta-fish style, only a piece of glass separating them from killing each other.

"You are not going to work at Checkers," Mom yelled. "So whatever idea your little friends have put in your head, just forget about it."

Molly's little friends, we'll call them Sherry and Karen, were goths from her AP classes. Though Karen wasn't that little. She was gigantic really, donning an assortment of polyester muumuus and shaved hairstyles. Sherry was more of a curvy, petite Ren-fair goth, with corset cleavage and long black curls that could make any guy at BARF, the Bay Area Renaissance Festival, choke on a turkey leg. These two already worked the Checkers fry basket. They'd already shown up at our house to cart Molly off to Denny's and Dungeons & Dragons games in cars that looked as beat down as Mom's. Needless to say, Molly was basically hired at Checkers. All she had to do was turn in the paperwork. But she wasn't eighteen, and she didn't have Mom's approval.

"One month," Molly said, counting down to her birthday.

"Over my dead body," Mom said.

"Oh, is that all it takes?"

❦

My mother always said the world did not revolve around us kids, but all that month I found myself next door on Andrea's trampoline, the moon and ghostly clouds gravitating toward us. Molly and Mom's screams wafted in and out of the house next door like a Hole album on a muffled boom box. My sister had it easy. She would escape in a few months, but I was only fourteen, years of school and awkwardness ahead of me. Andrea already had a Nissan Sentra waiting in the backyard for her. Andrea, who'd stopped playing Barbies to become one overnight, flexible and inexorably thin, with overdeveloped boobs and a perkiness that seemed invented by horny men. We alternated jumping on her trampoline and sitting in her Sentra as she started the vehicle, accelerated to an inch from cracking her family's aboveground pool, and then backed up. We could do this for hours, jolting forward and backward as she learned to shift, however long it took until her mom came out, wearing a parakeet or two, the schnauzers all over her feet like Ugg boots, saying, *Don't you think that's about enough?*

It never was.

We could sit on the trampoline all night, had done so before, listing off the boys at school who were borderline boyfriend material, borderline personality disorder. She went for the homies, the thugs, the guys with greasy hair who drove Berettas through the student parking lot at fifty miles an hour and left for lunch to get stoned. Guys who really did want to date her, guys who went out of their way to say *wassup* in the hall or flip her a note folded up so small it looked like a hit of acid. Guys who'd eventually follow her to community college, ask her to marry them, and fuck it up somehow when their jobs at Best Buy never panned out or they went to prison for dealing ecstasy or cheated.

"Justin Case," she whispered toward the sky. "God, let him break up with that ho."

For me, there was only Kyle. He looked like professional surfer Pat O'Connell and ran the Surf Club at school. When I saw him in the halls, my face would heat up and I'd want to die because I knew how cool he was, and how cool I wasn't. Everyone in the Surf Club lived on the water, had a boat, and knew how to wakeboard. It probably should've been called the Wakeboard Club. I just had stacks of *Surfer* magazines, a few pairs of Roxy shorts from Ross Dress for Less, and one Guy Harvey shirt. Kyle only hung out with juniors like Kristin Lavoie, who was head cheerleader and always elected to homecoming court, and even though she said hi to me in the halls, it was only because I used to be best friends with her little sister, Jen, before she lost all her eyelashes and had to leave school to live in a special care facility for people with eating disorders.

"Kyle," I whispered toward the sky. Then, as if by fate, my sister opened the back door at my house and yelled, "Phone call for you. It's some guy named Aaron."

Suddenly there was no fighting going on at my house. Everyone was quiet, gathered around the television as I locked myself inside my bedroom.

Aaron was Kyle's best friend. Not as cool, but still an okay member of the Surf Club and the swim team. He wanted to know the geometry homework since he'd missed it. Yeah, sure. We talked about the new issue of *Surfer*, how cool Rob Machado's 'fro was, which Malloy brother was the gnarliest.

"Who is Aaron?" Mom asked after.

"Yeah, who is Aaron?" Molly said.

"Nobody," I said, and Molly smiled so hard Mom actually reached over and touched her leg, both of them laughing.

The day Molly turned eighteen she handed in her Checkers application without telling Mom. She showed up with her new uniform, new hat, and name tag. Not a day later, Sherry and Karen were hanging out in the driveway, their faces seemingly marred by Sharpie, their mouths stuffed with cigarettes.

Mom wasn't so much irate now as out of control. She cried and tried to scare Molly straight. "If you think you're zitty now," she screamed into the glass door, "wait till you see what that grease can do."

Sometimes she could be right.

Fortunately, the I-was-just-flour-bombed-by-PETA look was in with the goths, so Molly covered her sebaceous face in albino makeup. She bought a vintage fur coat at Goodwill. One evening while I was listening to Dick Dale and reading about the art of tube riding, my sister appeared in the living room, her beautiful red hair slicked back and dyed black at the ends, freckles drowned in white foundation, eyes ringed in charcoal, lips like slivers of beet. Underneath her outfit appeared to be a second skin made entirely of black mesh.

"I turned Mom's old fishnets into a shirt," she said.

"Congratulations."

There was a flicker of light in the driveway, a car pulling in, and Molly was out the door.

"Where are you going?"

"Where do you think I'm going?"

When Mom got home, she was furious. "Where is she? Where did she go?"

"Probably to Denny's."

We were out the door then, driving down Highway 19, past the shitty tattoo parlors and strip clubs, to the Denny's on Trouble Creek, where Molly, Sherry, and Karen stood in the parking lot with a bunch of other kids who looked like a casting call for *Hellraiser*. A couple were hunched over on the curb in their shiny black outfits like vinyl records warped by heat. Some leaned against Geo Metros and palm trees. There were flasks and Big Gulps being passed around. There was Sherry in her corset, her body like a ketchup packet when you squeeze it so hard on top all the contents fall to the bottom. Karen in her sequined dress and black overcoat like some hobo Liza Minnelli.

"Get in the car," Mom yelled.

Molly crossed her arms. She was pressed up against a skinny kid from school with blue hair; the dye had stained his scalp and forehead in the manner of a swirlie victim.

"What are you doing?" Molly said. She gave me the evil eye. I'd ratted on her, and I'd been forced to drive along to the scene of the crime and point her out. There, the perpetrator, and here, the narc sinking toward the floor, where she could disappear beneath a sea of old banana peels as hard and dark as shoehorns. And the roaches. Oh, the roaches.

"Get inside this car right now!" Mom screamed, but Molly wouldn't budge.

Mom got out then. I begged her not to. The wagon was also known to die when it wanted to die, which was every time Mom took her foot off the gas. The engine sputtered, gasping for breath.

"Who do you think you are dragging my daughter out on a school night?" Mom yelled at Karen. "You think this makes you cool, smoking cigarettes in front of this shit hole?"

"No, ma'am," Karen said, blowing smoke from the side of her mouth. There were a few nervous chuckles.

"Don't talk back to me, you little smart-ass," Mom said, and I felt bad then, for all of us, causing a scene in a Denny's parking lot, even the car ready to die.

"Just leave us alone, Mom!" Molly shrieked. She started crying, and I could see something about Karen's face then too, and then Sherry's. Something was off; all their makeup was smeared. They'd all been crying or something.

"Leave!" Molly screamed again.

"I'm not going anywhere until you get in the damn car."

"No. I'm eighteen."

"It's fine, just go," Karen said.

"I'm sorry," Mom sniped. "Since when do you control what my daughter does?"

"Fuck off, crazy lady!" Karen screamed. "God, I can't deal with this right now."

"Are you on drugs or something?" Mom screamed. "What's wrong with you?"

"Her mother just died," Molly said. "She just wants to be

around her friends. Her mother just died from cancer. Is that okay with you?"

The station wagon let out a low guttural rumble. I searched for the gas pedal but my foot didn't make it in time. The car shook hard, violently, and finally broke down.

After that, my mother spent her days accompanying John on manic buying sprees to Sam's Club and building a barricade around her bedroom out of magazines, towels, carpet samples, and folded laundry. Molly emerged from her habitat only to be whisked away in cars covered in Tool and Prick bumper stickers. Otherwise she hid behind the large swaths of tissue paper she'd taped up on the sliding glass. In the evening lamplight they turned diaphanous, and she traipsed about to Tori Amos or the Cure, doing her sad dances like a silhouette in the window of a red-light district.

"I can see you in there, Bubbles," I'd tell her from the couch. "Come dance for Lisa Marie, baby."

But she didn't care. She didn't want to watch MTV or eat microwaved nachos with any fourteen-year-olds. She just sat in her room listening to her music. She'd inherited Mom's ability to hold a grudge, to stretch out the guilt treatment so long it finally bloomed into resentment. She went and got an eyebrow piercing, but Mom didn't even punish her or anything.

"Well, I hope you don't end up with hepatitis," was all Mom said into the glass.

Mom didn't even argue when Molly called up Grandma and asked for part-time custody of the Dodge Colt.

"Oh, sure, Miss Molly," Grandma said. She had an extra car, several if you counted the vehicular graveyard in the back field. "Just be careful." We all knew how she herself drove. The Colt was a half-breed—neither wagon nor minivan—and pretty much lamer than an El Camino, a labradoodle, or even that Cher song about some squaw's bastard child, but Molly was glad to drive the shit out of that poor car. There was no reason she needed to be nice to me, to allow me to ride shotgun, but she did. I was thrilled to accompany her. It had very little horsepower, not what you'd expect from a car named after a strapping young uncastrated horse. We believed we had balls anyways: windows down, seats reclined, feet on the cracked dash, 98 Rock blasting Metallica as we stuck our heads out the windows and yelled at kids who had to walk to school, their shoulders dislocated by heavy JanSports, their instrument cases hovering like censor bars. *Sleep with one eye open*, we warned them, *gripping your pillow tight*.

There were nights when Molly skipped out on her free Denny's coffee refills and drove us to the empty Baptist church parking lot in downtown New Port Richey, long after the Kelly Bells had gone home from their youth groups, no souls in sight. She let us switch seats and I'd drive around the parking lot and then take to the dark streets myself. I drove around Orange Lake, which was no bigger than a retention pond, and probably really was a retention pond, where each winter they set up life-size Christmas cards painted by the sick and elderly. We'd go around the loop and look for the one with the squirrel on it because it was the one we liked best.

My sister hauled us all around town. Driving nowhere,

driving endlessly. Cruising through our family's old fishing camp, Baillie's Bluff, which had been a hub of the fishing industry in the late 1800s, way before the touristy Sponge Docks, until a hurricane swept it away. Now it was a neighborhood with gigantic beautiful houses that had the only view of the sunset in town. We gawked at their lavish yards, their new cars. We had schoolmates who lived out here with bedrooms bigger than our whole house. You had to take your shoes off to walk inside. We kept going, driving through our family's old cow pastures, now Holiday Lake Estates. We had friends who lived in these houses too, some where you couldn't take your shoes off inside without having fleas devour both your feet.

We were desperate to explore, see something new, have some great life-affirming moment. It was something like *Thelma & Louise*, except we weren't that old and deranged yet and the person in the backseat wasn't Brad Pitt but gum-smacking Andrea, who came along only because we promised to drive by Justin Case's house and see if he was outside using his ho. He never was. A few weeks of this type of freedom, and Grandma's voice was on the answering machine: *Hello, Miss Molly, I'm sorry, but I need the car back tomorrow.*

A month or so before school ended, I came home from track practice to find John in the dining area. He was home sick and tinkering around with our ancient computer instead of resting.

"Have you heard of something called AOL?" he asked me.

"No." I had no idea what he was talking about, nor did I care.

I made my nachos, watched MTV in my bedroom. Suddenly there was a knock on the front door and the sound of John's chair screeching across the floor. He tapped on my bedroom door.

"There are some boys here to see you. Aaron and Kyle?"

"What?" I said. I almost gagged. I had on my smelly running clothes and cheese food stuck in my braces.

I walked out to the living room and found them there, standing around awkwardly among our junk. Our mismatched couches and chairs, our never-vacuumed rug, and a television from the 1980s on a sagging bookcase, weighed down by books, tchotchkes, and dead flowers. Our Jazzercise paint job, our plethora of dusty baskets, and John pinned between the dining table and the computer table saying, "Hey, fellas, you ever heard of AOL?"

"I was driving around with Kyle," Aaron said. "So we thought we'd stop in. I told you we might stop by after swim practice this week, right?"

"I thought you were, like, joking."

"Well, we're in the neighborhood. We gotta go to K-Mart to get some shrimping boots, if you want to go."

"Why do you need shrimping boots?"

"Because we just do," Aaron said, and they both laughed.

It was wrong. It was all wrong. I wanted Kyle to close his eyes, to not see the way the sheet was slumping off of John's old couch, revealing its ugly brown plaid, or the mismatched pillows and dust bunnies and unhung artwork. I wanted them to leave here, and then I wanted to go back in my bedroom and die. Or listen to Bonnie Raitt songs and cry into my Snoopy pillowcase. Either would work.

"Do you want to come with us?"

"Um, okay," I said. "John, is it cool if I go with them?"

John, who had never been allotted any form of authority in his life, looked at me very confused. "I don't know. I guess so."

Then I was in the back of Kyle's car, sucking nacho out of my teeth, not able to hear anything over the Sprung Monkey tape. Kyle had a very nice car, nicer than Mom's or John's. The back of his head was soft and white like dandelion down, and everything smelled just as I imagined it would, of coconut and Tahitian vanilla. He had expensive wraparound sunglasses you could only get at the surf store in the mall, and he had a special device for opening his garage door clipped to his sun visor, because people like Kyle didn't keep their cars parked outside while junk piled up in the garage. People like Kyle parked where they were supposed to park, and doors just magically opened for them too.

I don't know why they brought me to K-Mart. There weren't even any shrimping boots there. I was scared of opening my mouth, the dumb words that might spill out. There was a fake cardboard computer in the electronics section with a card-board keyboard that Aaron picked up.

"Hey, guys. Have you heard of AOL?"

Kyle laughed and I laughed, but I didn't think it was that funny. Not really. I thought of the embarrassment of it all. How I knew Kyle thought nothing of me, and probably never would, not after seeing inside my house and having an up-close look at my teeth.

We went to the other K-Mart, in Tarpon Springs, passing the strip malls and cinder-block houses mercuried by dusk.

We passed the power plant and Superfund site on the back road. Passed the Sponge Docks and the saw grass, the entire world swallowed by a burned-dinner scent. But no shrimping boots could be found.

Aaron turned down the music on the ride back home. "What's up, Knappy? You've been pretty quiet."

"Nothing," I said. "I just have a feeling I'm probably going to get in trouble."

"Bummer," Kyle said. He had nothing in the world to be bummed about. He blasted Blink-182 and kept his sunglasses on, though it was too dark to actually need them.

The sky seemed practically squeezed from a blood orange, as if we lived in a fireball, or Hades itself, with our swarming night clouds of flies and mosquitoes and parking lot seagulls. We flew down Highway 19, past the Checkers, where despite the mile-long line of minivans waiting for their Big Bufords and chocolate shakes, the goths had converged in the parking lot for their hourly clove break. They leaned on their cars, ruling over their small greasy empire completely indignant at the world around them.

There, my sister leaned against her own car. She'd saved enough money to buy a shiteous Honda from our family friend Bruce, who had a backyard full of cars that, like him, barely worked. It was a turd-brown hatchback, born the same year as me, 1981, covered in atrocious bumper stickers. *Subvert the dominant paradigm* and *The end of civilization will be from civilization itself.* She drove that thing all over the place, to the Castle in Ybor City, to the State Theatre in St. Pete, to Denny's, to work. In a few months she'd drive it up to Gainesville to go to college. She was completely free.

When I got back home nobody was there. Andrea came running over in the yard, watching the boys pull out of the driveway.

"No way," she said. "Your mom came over to our house and was asking where you were. She was so pissed. You are going to be in so much trouble."

"Where did she go?"

"I don't know, like, Boston Market or something. Did I tell you? Justin Case dumped that ho. I got a note."

"You did?"

"Yeah, you want to read it?"

"Maybe later," I said.

I didn't ask her inside. I took a shower and washed my hair. I brushed my teeth and used a special brush the size of a mascara wand to get all the nachos out from in between my braces. I went to my sister's room and tried on her clothes and jewelry. Put on her Smashing Pumpkins, pushed the novels off her bed. *The bitterness of one who's left alone,* Billy Corgan wailed. I buried myself under her blankets and closed my eyes. There was the faintest trace of cigarette, burger, and Sunflowers perfume on my sister's pillow. I stuffed it over my face, enough to suffocate just a little.

After a While You Just Get Used to It

I t was Thanksgiving, and we were heading to Grandma's place, just past Aunt Ruby's house, which, like most things in Florida, had ended up a used-car lot. We cruised down Grand Boulevard in Mom's gigantic boat, which she'd "inherited" from John's uncle Dale the year I went to college and then deemed it her "cop car." There was a general slowing of traffic in front of us everywhere we went, it's true, but that could've easily been blamed on the median age in Holiday, hovering somewhere between seventy and Methuselah.

Speaking of meth, from the younger, scabbier demographic up in Dixie County to the north, where the rebel flag was still flown over Highway 19 in between the Hardee's and a sign that told you how far away the state penitentiary was, Aunt Susie and her third husband, say his name was Ricky Haunch, had driven down for the holiday. Susie was coming off a couple weeks' jail time for minor infractions and no doubt looking for a relaxing weekend of binge drinking and seasonal sedatives. Turkey. Gravy. Oxycodone. An unfamiliar truck was in Grandma's driveway, jacked up too high to belong to anyone but them.

"Don't go near the damn thing," Mom said.

But the queen of telling us what to do made the biggest mistake of all: opening the front door to Grandma's house without first knocking. One foot inside and her twenty-pound purse flew from her shoulder, spilling an arsenal of pens and panty liners across the floor as Aunt Susie's two blue heelers latched on to her right ankle with their teeth. They punctured her brown polyester pants near the hem while she worked them like a Skip-It, a toy I used to play with in the backyard of Aunt Ruby's; people in cars would stop and stare as I swung around the child-sized version of a real-life ball and chain.

It took four people and fifteen curse words to restrain the dogs, Susie and Ricky to pull them off, and Grandma to swat around her kitchen towel as if putting out a fire.

"Of course the goddamn dogs bit Margie," Jack said. "They've been trained by Susie."

Mom disappeared to the bathroom and wrapped her bites in rolls of gauze that had been in the drawer so long they'd aged like the teeth of coffee drinkers. The whole house filled with the scent of the Designer Imposters perfume my cousin Beth, Uncle Jack's oldest daughter, stashed in there when she lived with Grandma for two weeks back in 1989, right after she stole a bunch of money from the video store where she worked. It was her rebel scent. And mine as well, for back in the day, I'd come over and douse myself with the yellow can of it, spraying the aerosol all over my clothes and prancing to the kitchen to steal away some Easter crackle chocolates that lived beneath a squirrel tail and an envelope filled with human hair in the junk drawer. I finally stopped when the Designer Imposters turned the front of my Hypercolor shirt a deep bruise shade the shape of Russia.

"I wish she'd left those damn dogs at home," Grandma told me and Molly. "One already shit on the bed in the back bedroom."

"One tinkled on the floor in here," Grandma's sister, Aunt Mickey, yelled from the living room, already cleaning it. Aunt Mickey loved to clean. She carried enough cleaning products in the back of her car to kill off any potential passengers under the age of four.

"I'm not sure we should stay," Mom said, hobbling into the kitchen. "I don't feel comfortable after being attacked."

"You goddamn well better stay," Grandma said. "We have farting monkeys. Jack, get the farting monkeys."

A gag gift from Walgreens appeared then and was passed around to fart away our sorrows. Soon Susie and Ricky emerged from the front bedroom, their dogs locked up inside.

"Margie, I'm sorry," Susie said, leaning in for a hug. Mom tried to deny her at first but then relented. They were, after all, sisters. Pretty much identical when you got past all the hangups and right down to the bad tempers and doughy faces.

"It's okay," Mom said. "How are you doing?"

"Oh, me?" Susie said. "I'm fine."

She had lost more teeth than last time though. Arms scabbier. Hair stringier. Her voice a gravel road. She and Ricky both

wore the same kind of flannel shirt, the same kind of Wranglers that had stopped fitting right after years of weight loss.

"Somebody get me a beer," Mom demanded. She didn't
want one to drink. She took it unopened into the living room
and propped her foot up, letting the beer ice her ankle.

"I got just the thing for you," Ricky told her, which was the
sort of thing you never wanted Ricky Haunch saying to you.
One time at a family Easter egg hunt years back, he'd whispered something in Mom's ear while nobody was looking and
she'd spent the entire afternoon in a quiet rage, finally cursing
him on the drive home. She never would tell us what Ricky
Haunch had said. *It doesn't need repeating,* she'd said after we
kept pressing her, *so shut it.*

He went and retrieved a large medicine bag, dropping it on
the coffee table. It was as big as the Elizabeth Arden makeup
bags John got Mom every Christmas with a $200 cosmetic pur-
chase, no matter how broke he was. Ricky Haunch procured
my mother a single Aleve.

"Thank you," she said.

"Ain't that cool, girls?" he said, showing off his bag. We'd
come to watch Aunt Mickey shampoo the carpet, to see the
dramatic before-and-after pee-stain removal, not to sneak a
peek at his stash. "Susie found this at a flea market over there
in Old Town."

"Wouldn't be the first time she found herself some flea-
bag," Uncle Jack said, hauling in the farting monkeys for a
special encore performance.

❦

I'm not sure when it was that I first realized there might be something wrong with my aunt Susie. By the time I was born, she'd already long ago dropped out of college and gone through a succession of bikers as if devouring them wendigo style. Two abusive husbands by age thirty-five. Too many scars to count. I'd dumped a basket of rose petals all over the aisle at her second wedding, in my grandparents' backyard, but I never recognized anything out of the ordinary early on. Her second husband was a guy named Jay with a ZZ Top beard and leather vests for days. They'd lived in my great-grandma's old house, next door to my grandparents. I recall chickens, cats, a hacking cough that carried over the orange trees into Grandma's yard on the evening wind. She managed to hold down her job at Grandma's bookkeeping business, even as her teeth started to fall out. Maybe they got knocked out. Who knows.

There came a night at our house on Dixie Highway when the wendigo herself flew into the yard, howling for my mother, pulling on the screen door so hard it ripped off the hinges. She beat on the back door, screaming in tongues, pleading for Mom to let her in. I lay in bed with the covers over my face, my sister frozen in the top bunk, terrified.

"Susie?" my mother said through the door. "What's going on?"

"They're coming to get me. They're coming, Margie!" she screamed. "I'm in fucking trouble. Help me."

Months before, a drunk guy had wandered over from the volleyball bar down the street in the middle of the night and punched out the window over my mother's sleeping head. The glass shattered all over her bed as she screamed bloody murder. The cops had found him passed out near our rabbit pens, his arms soaked in blood. Our grandparents had to come get us so we could sleep at their place, and we saw him slumped in the back of the squad car. He looked like Buddy from *Charles in Charge*—a tan, nerdy guy with a curly mullet hairdo and a button-down shirt tucked into his jeans. Aunt Susie looked like nobody who would ever star on a television show. She had the reckless, abandoned eyes of people raised by wolves and could count the number of times she'd stepped foot in a mall or donned panty hose and dress shoes on one hand alone.

She was from a darker place. The place the volleyball bar had been before some asshole dumped sand on the sandspur patch of land he'd bought off our family and called it a good time. She was from backwoods Florida, land of crackers, of ancestors, of roads paved with shell, of Calusa Indian burial grounds and trailers that filled up with wasps and bees if you let them sit in the backyard too long. The fear this very woman put into me. My relative, somebody whom I could grow up to be just like, the beast of it in my blood, was at the back door, and she was wanting in.

My mother ducked her head into our room.

"It's okay, girls," she said. "It's just Susie."

Then she let her sister rip through the house, a wild animal immediately wanting back out. *They're crawling on me*, she screamed, *they're crawling all over me, Margie, help me!* There was nothing crawling on her skin. Before she went running out the front door, there was only this: my mother convincing her younger sister to calm down in the bedroom attached to our own, the light shining on the bunk bed from the crack in the door, my mother holding on to Susie with two hands. There was blood all over her, blood on the carpet, blood on the door. Her shirt no longer looked like a shirt. It was torn, hanging like a papoose.

"At least put on a shirt!" Mom screamed as Susie swung open the front door. She made it a quarter mile down Dixie Highway, running toward her house, when the cops picked her up, and we slowly made it back to sleep, the shock of it all fading from our bodies like a million needles being removed one by one.

After that came the infractions, the drunk-and-disorderlies, the altercations, the Golden Nugget, the Sponge Dock dives, the borrowing of money from unsavory roadhouse types. It's not that she was an idiot. She was actually quite smart. When she punched out that lady in the movie theater for talking too loud, the film she was trying to watch was *The Piano*, which was at least on the cerebral side. She read voraciously, often made it through all the paperbacks in jail long before her sentence was over. In terms of accounting, she could keep the books with the best of them. Hell, you didn't need all your fingernails to use a calculator, or to find love either. Ricky Haunch came around one Easter after she got out of lockup and stuck around like rotten on egg. He moved into her house and threw all her ceramic roosters to the floor, and then her furniture, and then Susie herself. There had been bad coked-up fights, too many to count, but then they'd made up and snuck off and gotten married, not telling anybody until a year later.

To say that my family hated Ricky would be an understatement. To say Grandma hadn't threatened to kill him by shotgun in her driveway during hunting season 1995 would be a lie. So he'd moved Susie up to a place in Dixie County, away from her job, away from her family, to a place where nobody could see what was going on anymore, to a place where nobody could hear her, or take note, or be much concerned. My family was tapped out, done with getting hung up in her drug abuse and craziness.

When my family gathered for a holiday, any holiday, it was always the same. There were snacks on the kitchen table while Grandma or Jack did the cooking, there were beer and wine in various coolers, and the only means of communication was getting drunk and screaming, more commonly referred to as getting 'er done.

In the living room, Mom had found her voice again, reliving every moment of her attack story as if starring in a *Hard Copy* segment. She took everyone through what happened, though nobody asked her to and nobody was listening but Mickey, who was now Windexing the giant sliding glass doors, and John, who told her, "You need to go to the doctor. You might need a rabies shot."

"Shit, John, you should get one too," Jack said. "If you've been kissin' Margie all these years."

Relatives poured into the kitchen at the first cracking-open of beer like house cats lured by the can opener. The family hunting buddies, Deon and Bruce, stopped off with venison sausage from a buck Grandma had shot up in Gulf Hammock a week before. Family friends and relatives whom I had no desire to count the teeth of were there too, talking about the new gator-hunting lottery and how sad it was that all the Kenny Rogers Roasters had closed. We gathered around my grandma as she cut up taters to scallop, enjoying ourselves, until Ricky Haunch wandered in like a red tide.

"Well, Susie locked herself in the bedroom," he said. "And she says she ain't coming out unless I leave. She's all mad because I invited Ricky Junior over."

Ricky Junior apparently hadn't seen Ricky in several years. He wasn't his real son, of course. Mom loved to tell the story of how his real dad, Ricky's best friend, had gone off and gotten killed in Vietnam. Ricky had raised the boy as his own, married the kid's mom, who was his best friend's high school sweetheart, long vanished herself. Mom always got a strange look about her whenever she talked about the boys she knew who went to Vietnam and never came back.

Grandma stopped cutting potatoes and pointed her long knife right in his direction. "You two can knock it off, or I'll kick both of you out."

Ricky Haunch threw his hands up like *I ain't doing shit* and retreated to the back porch to smoke. Then the family was back at it, holding four simultaneous conversations at once. Cousin Debbie's girls' gymnastics team went to state, while Jeb Bush's crackhead daughter got sent to rehab. A barracuda jumped into some guy's boat out near Anclote Key and bit a chunk of his thigh off, and two horses were swallowed by a sinkhole and drowned over in Osceola when a water pipe burst.

There was a hierarchy here, with the older relatives usually being the wiser and loudest, usually ending a conversation or story in *no, goddamn it,* while the youngest, myself included at twenty-one years of age, were often regarded as half mutes sent to fetch the elders their beverages.

Uncle Jack, as the middle child and loudest of all, was an exception to the hierarchy, having obviously taken a better approach starting back in junior high, when he first brought home the tuba to practice over his family's conversations in the next room.

It was cacophonous, ear piercing, and annoying. *Don't worry,* you might warn a newcomer, some bewildered boyfriend or classmate you'd invited and would never hear from again, *after a while you just get used to it.* First came beer, then came the dirty jokes. Once the first jug of wine was finished, the racist diatribes and Burl Ives impersonations reared their ugly heads like gophers in need of malleting. Sometimes Grandma would tell a great story—when she jumped off the roof of her house like Mary Poppins with an umbrella and broke her nose; when she watched two of her younger siblings mowed down by a bus in Mexico—but usually, conversation just deteriorated into debates about family folklore, so there could be no way to clarify the factuality or authenticity of arguments surrounding such statements as *I'll tell you the real reason that oak in the front yard is called the Hanging Tree.* God help you if you made eye contact with anybody having a heated debate, as that was akin to picking sides in a battle nobody can win. You would never live it down.

"Well you took Jack's side," Mom would say later. "That my forehead's too big to have bangs this short."

"No, I didn't."

"Yes you did. I saw it with my own eyes."

It wasn't a holiday until my mother, and everybody else for that matter, had left Grandma's feeling victimized by their loved ones.

The turkey was cooling and the sides were almost done when Aunt Libby and her dog, Britches, a Maltese gimp with front legs like crabs' claws, finally arrived. The dog had been dying of congestive heart failure since it was born, with eye boogers for days and a cough like a lifelong smoker, always ridding himself of extraneous fluids on a nice carpet or doily. Britches was older than most folks who call pants *britches* and simply refused to die, happy as he was. My grandma once had a cat that, unlike Britches, was quite accurately named Boogeyfarts, and that animal knew when it was time to die. Went out back into the field toward the tall grass and dog pens and never returned. Britches could barely walk, let alone dream of escaping to the land of dead animals and vehicles out back.

"Oh, Aunt Libby, you're here," Mom said. "You won't believe what Susie's dogs did to my leg."

"Well, Britches wants to hear, don't you, Britches?"

Britches did not, having writhed out of Aunt Libby's grasp to wander the living room and snag his ingrown toenails every two feet.

"Well, where is Susie?" Aunt Libby asked.

"Oh, she's locked in the bedroom."

Not wanting to relive my mother's dog attack again, I headed to the kitchen. I was lurking by the cheese-and-meat plate when the rest of the family decided to flee the kitchen to show Aunt

Libby a set performed by the farting monkeys, leaving me alone with Ricky Haunch. He cracked open a Bud and stared.

"Seen them monkeys fart a dozen times already," he said.

His silver oil slick of hair was parted down the side and lopped over his forehead, which was as wind blasted and creviced as the untamed deserts of faraway lands. And that's where he should've been, somewhere far away from there. Not married to my aunt, not in Grandma's kitchen, not there, talking to me. He smiled at me now, knee-deep in a mouth of dry rot, all black gums and gray teeth. The sleeves of his flannel were rolled up and sores as dark and hard as jerky dotted his arms. Thick, blue veins ran beneath them like rivers that could wash away whole towns.

"How you doing, girly?" he asked, very sweet, too sweet.

"Me?" I said, spitting an olive pit into a napkin. "I'm fine."

"Well, good," he said, leaning back against the counter and smirking. "It's sure nice to see all you girls together, young and old."

"Yeah," I said, stuffing a piece of jalapeño jack cheese in my mouth.

"To me," Ricky Haunch said, "it looks like you're becoming the new leggy blonde of the family."

I was choking then, my eyes watering, a piece of jalapeño lodged in my throat.

"Oh, see here, you ate the damn pepper jack from hell," Uncle Jack said, hurrying back into the kitchen at the first sign of a victim. "I found that stuff over at a little bodega by the Waccamaw. Sue done fell through a glass table up at Mickey's first time she ate a piece."

By the time dinner was ready, it was apparent that Aunt Susie would not be coming out of the front bedroom.

"Just come eat with us," Mom said through the door, and then Jack, and then Grandma, but Susie wouldn't budge. I was called on to help Grandma in the kitchen, but she didn't seem that upset about Susie's behavior.

"She's having herself a tantrum," she said. "But we can just eat without her."

Rarely did Grandma show signs of her age into her seventies, cooking this giant meal, doing her crosswords and jigsaw puzzles, having just returned from Gulf Hammock, where she'd bagged two bucks. Sometimes she accidentally called me Molly, or Mom Susie, but now she reeled back a little and dropped the scalloped potatoes to the floor.

"Are you okay?" I asked her.

"Oh, I'm fine, dolly," she said. "I'm just being a klutz."

I'd never seen her be a klutz before. I'd never seen the floor cleaned in my lifetime. I'd seen my grandpa, rest his soul, move a bloody, dripping pig's head over it to boil down for hog's head cheese a dozen times. I'd seen random cat shit tracked through the side door, hairballs bigger than tumbleweeds, an army of tiny black ants moving across it like a licorice stream for the past decade.

"Well, come on," Grandma said. "Help me get them back in the pan."

She held the tray with two shark mitts swallowing her hands, and I used a spatula to spoon the scalloped potatoes back in.

"Look here," she said. "Only eat from this little part that didn't fall."

It was about the time Grandma sat down to say grace that the front bedroom door opened and then slammed shut two times like demons were being exorcised from the green shag.

"Lord, we thank you," my grandma said as Aunt Susie finally barged into the foyer and sneered in our direction. She had the medicine bag in one hand and a backpack in the other. "Thank you for this beautiful food, and this family, and everything we have to be thankful for, Lord."

The front door opened and slammed shut.

"Amen," Grandma said.

"Amen," we said, and dug in.

Out in the driveway Susie revved the truck, and Ricky downed a few bites before stepping outside. He came back in with his medicine bag a few moments later and disappeared to the bedroom. There was the sound of tires peeling out on the driveway, and Ricky returned to the dinner table cordial as can be. Nobody said a word about it.

After dinner, there was a lull in conversation and festivities, as digestion and sobriety set in. The television was tuned to some Bing Crosby movie, and beers were ingested more slowly now, folks taking to the couches in Grandma's living room, practically comatose. This was when the doorbell rang, and in walked a man and woman with a baby.

"Everyone," Ricky said, "this here is Ricky Junior, and his wife, Linda, and little baby Eleanor."

"Happy Thanksgiving," we said.

Baby Eleanor was set down on the freshly cleaned carpet to see the farting monkeys.

"Isn't she a doll?" Grandma said. She was, but there was something off about all of them. They were dirt-poor, you could tell, more poor than us.

It made me think of something else, something that really had nothing to do with Ricky Haunch and his family at all. A few days after that drunk guy had wandered from the volleyball bar and broken Mom's window all those years back, a woman had shown up in our yard at the house on Dixie Highway. This woman was carrying a baby, and she parked her old van over our dandelions, crushing them. She was poking around near the house when we stumbled upon each other at an open window.

"I don't mean to scare you," she said, her face very close to the screen. "But is your mommy or daddy home?"

Naturally, she *had* scared me. I ran and told Mom exactly what had happened, that a stranger had approached me in the bathroom window while I was teasing my bangs.

My mother was in the yard in a flash, as my sister and I ran out to see, hanging on the steps like yard cats. The woman was to be sacrificed at the hand of our stranger-danger overlord, and we rejoiced. The woman was small and dull with a short brown bob, not pretty like my mother, who, though lithe, stood like a tower of flowing blond perm in the Bahia grass. The woman explained that she was the wife of the drunk guy who'd tried to break in. The little baby squirmed in her arms as she spoke. It cooed and drooled. She'd just come to check on the damage to our house, which was why she was looking around the yard.

"I just wanted to apologize," she said. "And see if there's anything I could do."

"You can get the hell off my property before I call the cops," Mom yelled in her face. The woman wasn't expecting that at all. She squirmed and the baby squirmed and they both released a sharp little wail, as if somebody had just jabbed them both in the side. I stopped smiling. I felt bad now, bad for wanting to see them hurt, bad as my mother shooed them from the lawn the way she did stray animals, salespeople, and Jehovah's Witnesses, with a stern *go on and get.*

"She just wanted to apologize," I said as they got back in the van.

"She was trespassing," Mom said. "Bringing a baby over here, can you just imagine?"

But I could tell she felt bad too. She didn't call the cops anyway. She sat on the bed and held her face in her hands, not crying, just stewing like she sometimes did.

I watched out the window as the woman started the van and merged back onto the road, going so slow it seemed like the entire world could pass her by, and maybe, eventually, it did.

Baby Eleanor clapped at the farting monkeys, and outside the sun set slowly, its famous orange glow draped over the world. We all enjoyed some pie, and when it was time to go, Ricky Haunch and his dogs loaded into the front of his son's little blue car. We waved them on toward the harsh light of the western sun.

The Great Give-and-Take

I wasn't there at her bedside like Mom was. I wasn't even in Florida. I was at my new home in North Carolina, about to drive to see this band Crooked Fingers play, when Mom called to tell me that Grandma had died. I was expecting it. She'd been moving in circles from her bed to the nursing home bed to the hospital bed with tangles of white cords coming out of her like tiny waterslides, like maybe her brain tumor would come shooting down a tube one day screaming *yeehaw*. But the brain tumor was large and round as a golf ball and wouldn't budge.

"It was peaceful," Mom told me. "But Susie didn't get to say good-bye. We tried to call her and tell her it was Mommy's time, but we don't know where she is."

What was there to say? *Call every bar they got up in Dixie County?*

"Go ahead to your concert," Mom told me. "Go be with your friends and then we'll get you a flight tomorrow. Okay?"

"Okay," I said. Except I didn't have many friends in my new town, and the music at the show was slow and quiet and the people all around drunk and loud. I couldn't hear the vocals at all. It was more difficult than listening to a twice-removed cousin's husband tell you about gator hunting while your grandma sings along to "Winter Wonderland" at Christmas dinner. Except she always sang it "Walking 'Round in Women's Underpants."

Two days later, I sat in Grandma's kitchen eating a piece of fudge as Susie moseyed in with her liquor store purchases. The wake was in two days, the funeral in three. Nobody knew if she would actually show up or not, but here she was, not doing well, not at all. She'd been diagnosed with hepatitis C—*hep C*, Mom kept calling it, like some new soda—but that hadn't stopped her from putting needles in her arms. She was going to prison any day now for well over a year; she'd gotten busted again on a DUI and possession charges after she ran out on Thanksgiving last year, her arms scabbier than I'd ever seen them.

"You want a shot?" she asked, taking her Goldschläger out of a brown bag. "There's real gold flakes in it."

"That's okay," I said.

I stole another piece of fudge from the dining table, where a festive tablecloth and holiday foods had been set up. It all looked so normal, the cheese and salami, the mini sandwiches and deviled eggs on a plastic tray, the cheddar popcorn in a giant Christmas tin. Greek families who my Grandpa did the books for had brought by grape leaves and koulourakia, and it was obvious people had been grazing all day. Everything else in the kitchen seemed different, sterile, counters devoid of fruit and bills and greasy pans. The whole house was this way. The Christmas tree should've been sealed in a bucket of cement Grandma style in the living room, the presents spilling all over the carpet. Instead, the room was bare as could be. Everywhere, the good meat had already been picked from the bone.

The curtain had been removed from the kitchen window, and you could see clear out in the side yard, to where my uncle Jack was running over from his house next door, as he had the day my grandpa died. He appeared just beyond the kitchen's French door, stomping over the brick patio Grandma had laid by hand just so she could sit in the fading sun every evening, enjoying her irises.

"Open it!" he screamed, beating on the door. He pulled the knob so hard, I thought it would break off. "Open it!" he screamed again. I obeyed. The door swung hard and cracked against the wall, panes of glass shattering across the floor.

He got her by the neck then. Aunt Susie. Choking her. Her face darkened to the deep color of her scabbed arms. A hoarse, curdling whine came from the space between her good teeth. It was all happening so fast. I had never seen his temper flare like this. I knew he had my grandfather's temper—they all did—but I'd never seen it in action. I still had a mouthful of fudge.

"Stop it, Jack," Susie pleaded.

"You think you can come up in Mommy's house and shoot that crap into your arms?"

"No." She punched him in the side, which didn't do anything but make him angrier.

My mom was on them in a flash, running in from the living room.

"Stop it!" she screamed. "This is Mommy's house."

"You stay out of this," Jack said.

"Not in Mommy's house," my mother yelled. She had a dish towel, and she swung it around just like my grandma would have. "Stop it, Jack."

He let Susie go then. She gasped, grasping at the counter, sinking low onto the floor, which was almost spotless now. Someone had scrubbed away all its personality, its years of seasoning, like taking steel wool to a cast-iron skillet. You could still see the history of stains in places, some of the grime humanly impossible to clean. How it lingered and ran together, forming a map of the past, where pots boiled over, where accidents and spills had happened and mistakes were made.

"Don't bring none of that crap to the services," Jack said. "Don't bring Ricky Haunch either. I'm bringing a shotgun with me. I mean it."

Then he put an arm around me as if nothing had happened. "Well, hey there, Wendy. How was your flight?"

"Good," I said. "It was good."

"Glad you got in okay. If you want a beer, there's a cooler full right here, and at our house too. Come on by."

Susie was bleeding in places, some of her scabs knocked loose in the scuffle, but she was trying to shake it off. She smiled the half-toothed smile of the forever abused and pulled us both out a beer. "Well, go on and have one," she said. "Welcome home."

❧

When my grandmother had first had the stroke, a week before I graduated college, Uncle Jack took her to the doctor. MRIs and CAT scans revealed she had a brain tumor, but Jack and Grandma kept it a secret for months. We'd gone to Macaroni Grill after my graduation and nobody could understand a thing Grandma said. Her tongue was basically paralyzed in her mouth. Still she smiled and drank wine. She held my hand and beamed, still radiant in her lavender blouse and matching hair ribbon. She drew beautiful flowers on the paper tablecloth with the complimentary crayons the hostess gave our table, while inside she was dying and didn't want any of us to know.

One secret she had taken to the grave: a heap of credit card debt that nobody had known the extent of. The house and car would have to be sold immediately, the belongings parceled out quickly to get things under way. My mother had already taken her share and more. Boxes of photos and linens and ancient rusty tools now covered the floor. Furniture was stacked on furniture. Out back, Grandma's irises and orchids lay across the ground, ready to be replanted.

There was no way to get around at the house on Missouri Avenue. I couldn't even squeeze into the garage to see Mom's ballet slippers, a secret ritual I'd always had every time I visited home. When I was in sixth grade my feet barely fit into these slippers. Her feet had been that small in college. I'd cram my feet into the slippers and try to go up on my toes like I was meant to star in *Swan Lake*. I couldn't do it. It hurt so much. I couldn't take half the pain. I put the shoes back and pretended I'd never seen them. My toes bruised and I wore socks so Mom wouldn't see. She wanted her old things around, but she never wanted you to touch them.

"Do I go mess with all your things?" she'd ask me when she caught me dressed in her old purple hot pants or a velvet minidress, when I had out her old photo albums or her old records. Her life before motherhood seemed so mysterious and wonderful. I couldn't resist any of it.

But now she was digging around in all *her* mom's old things. Maybe things her mom wouldn't want her to touch.

"What are you doing with all of Grandma's things like this?" I asked her after one look at the house. "What do you want with all of this? You have a severe problem."

"No. I. Don't," she said, doing her lip-pinch, like a butthole scowl. "Everyone acts like I'm crazy and I'm not. I know this is a lot of stuff, but so what? It's my life. It's not some joke, so stop laughing."

"I'm sorry," I said. I couldn't help but laugh. I was standing in an empty box because it was the only place left for me to stand.

The next day, Mom stood over me as I snoozed on the last remaining couch in Grandma's living room, urging me to come look at some plates. "This is the only time you have to get things you may want, and you're just going to nap all day?"

"Yup."

"Don't you want things to remember your grandmother by?"

I did, but I already had them. My grandma gave me my first squirrel, a saltshaker, when I was in high school. I wish I could show her my collection today. Let her touch all the pieces, and laugh at some, and hear her say, *Ohhh, he's a handsome squirrel, isn't he, dolly?* After graduation from college, she'd given me my own quilt and matching pillowcases to take up to North Carolina. My own braided rug for the kitchen, my own coffee mug collection, a Japanese jewelry box. I had no interest in spending the entire day taking inventory of her last remaining possessions. I woke up hours later and Molly was in Grandma's closet, having finally arrived from New Orleans.

"Do you want any of these purses?" she asked.

"I guess," I said, sprawling across Grandma's bed. Her romance books were gone, the topless Fabios hauled off for other old ladies to caress.

"Well get off your ass and come look at them," she said.

"What's wrong with you?"

"Nothing." But I already knew. My sister had been exposed to Mom for more than ten minutes, and now her usual three-step process—the Bitch Treatment, as I liked to call it—was happening: a brief and silent rage, loud venting, and nonstop chain-smoking. Molly was clearly in the rage stage. Like Mom, she enjoyed the meditative quality of resentment as it pressure-cooked you from the inside out.

"She's just really pissing me off," she said after a few minutes.

"Shocking."

"I guess I'm an asshole for telling Sherry I'd meet her out tonight instead of staying in and listening to Mom whine about Jack and Susie. God, I'm such a horrible person."

"She's under a lot of stress." From the sound of it, she was handling the kitchen pack-up the way a velociraptor might handle searching for children in the cabinets and oven.

"I'm going to smoke a cigarette," Molly said.

In the kitchen, Mom was going through pots now.

"She's going through pots now," Mr. Obvious told me.

"Thanks, John. I see that."

"Do you need pots?" Mom asked.

"I don't know. Not really."

"Take this one," she said. "They don't make pots like this anymore."

Not since child labor laws were passed in the twentieth century anyways. I put my pot on the counter. The start of a stack I should've already been working on hours ago. Molly watched us through the window, smoking up a storm. She pulled a flask out of her bag and waved it in the air, flicking around her long Gene Simmons tongue.

"Mom, how long do you think we're going to be here?"

"Yeah, Margie," John said. "I'm starting to get hungry."

"Until I get through everything I need to get through, okay?" She was not asking nicely. "You haven't even looked through anything," she hissed at me.

She held up a small orange cast-iron pan for me to see, and I put it beside my pot. Then my mother handed me two ancient cast-iron skillets, and suddenly I had a collectible-skillet stack building.

"Margie, I'm real hungry," John whined.

"Then have some goddamn snacks, John."

He unscrewed the top of a plastic jug and grabbed a handful of stale cheese balls. "But I need some real lunch, not a bunch of crap."

"Then go get some. Nobody is stopping you."

"Fine," he said. He tucked in his Margaritaville shirt, felt the back of his shorts for his wallet, and awaited his orders from the Sarge, but they never came. "Well, what do you want me to get?"

"Whatever," Mom said. She was more concerned with the skillets, the Pyrex, the dusty wok with two dead roaches in it.

"Why don't you go get some subs from Publix," I said, hoping to appease everyone.

"No!" Mom screamed. "I don't want a sub."

"Well what do you want?"

She paused a moment to really think about it. She thought about it for a long time, too long, an indication that her own Bitch Treatment was afoot.

"How about," she screamed, "you all fuck off!"

John, following orders, immediately headed off in his truck. Tears ran down Mom's face then, and her chin cratered in places, deep as the moon. I'd never liked to see her cry, always found that it made me want to cry as well, and now I closed my eyes, trying not to think of my mom, or of Grandma, or of anything at all. I went in to hug her, but she pushed me away. She didn't want me touching her.

"I'm sorry," I told her.

A minute later, John pulled back up.

"I forgot my phone," he said, his voice a tiny island in the sea of my mother's telling him off. Then he was out the front door again. My sister threw a double sign of the horns and lit another cigarette.

"I need help, okay?" Mom said after a minute. She swung open a new cabinet and nosed around. "And none of you will help me. So fuck you people. Fuck you all." Her voice wavering, relenting. She didn't really mean it. She just didn't know any other way to react than by taking it out on us. It's just who she was.

"I'm trying to help," I told her.

"No, you're not. You'd rather lie on the couch. Are you going to sleep through her funeral too?"

"Jesus, Mom."

"I only have a specific amount of time today, because I wanted to go to the store and get something for dinner. But now John is gone for lord knows how freaking long, so we can't load the truck, and Molly isn't even going to have dinner because she has to go out with Sherry. So why the fuck should I care?"

"Mom."

"Wendy," she said mockingly. "Nobody cares about my feelings. Nobody cares how I feel."

"I do. I'm sorry, okay? I'm here. You're not exactly the easiest person to be around right now. You get all psycho and angry for no reason."

"My mother just died, if you didn't notice."

"I'm sorry, Mom. We loved her too, you know."

She was quiet for a moment, stewing, I thought, but then she huffed, "I'm sorry."

"Well, what do you want me to do?"

"Hold these," she said, handing me a stack of ugly tan bowls from the cabinet. Then she reached in and pulled out some bowls from the way back.

"Here," she said. "These are the ones I wanted you to see. I think you should have them." She held out two bowls with a couple of lederhosen-clad cartoon children about to kiss, a tiny squirrel peering out from between them. I put them on my stack.

"Call John," she said. "Tell him if he's picking up subs that I want the Cuban."

On the day of the wake, Aunt Susie called the house and asked for me. She wanted me to come over to Grandma's house because she had something for me. *Just go*, Mom said, and gave me her keys. I drove down to Holiday, past Gulf High and the miles of cement-block houses and strip malls that turned uglier each passing year. Past our old house on Dixie Highway turned used-car lot, past my great-grandma's house turned Knights of Columbus.

Somewhere out back I could hear Ricky Haunch running his mouth and some other men laughing, testing their luck within shooting range of Jack's house. Aunt Susie was in the back bedroom, where Mom and John had lived when we were homeless for a few months back in 1994.

"I found something in the garage that you should really have," she said. Given her history of work-glove and flashlight-keychain Christmas presents, I got a little scared. She led me to the kitchen and grabbed herself a beer from the cooler, then poked into the garage for a minute. She came back with a very old guitar, brown and dusty, the strings rusted and hanging loose from the body like power lines downed by heavy winds.

"Do you think you can play it?" she asked. "I don't know where it came from. None of us ever did play guitar. But it's real old. Might be worth something."

She handed it to me, and I wiped some dust away. I tightened up three strings, two of them completely broken and the other unable to move with the tuning key rusted in place. I played her a few wretched chords.

"Sounds like shit," she said. "You don't have to take it."

"No. I want it," I said. "Thank you."

I took it back to the house and cleaned the old thing. It sounded horrible, but I played anyways.

That evening, Aunt Susie avoided the entire family at the wake, slipping in toward the end of visiting hours, crying in the back row of the funeral home's parlor, and slipping back out. I felt bad for her. Nobody wanted her around, and Ricky was a no-show. The last time I'd seen her dressed up in a skirt and jacket was at her second wedding. She may very well have been wearing the same homely tan pumps.

"We're going to Mommy's," Mom said, heading off with

John. Molly and I had driven separately, hoping to flee early from my mother's nonstop schedule of poaching.

"We have all the food," Uncle Jack told us before we left. "So come to our house."

Molly and I went to Jack's and parked in his driveway. We went inside and sat down at the kitchen island, stuffing our faces with spanakopita and dips and desserts. Somebody poured us wine. Somebody served us cake. We'd been there for about ten minutes when there was a loud banging on the side door.

"Open it!" my mother screamed.

Jack obeyed, and the door swung hard.

"What the hell are you two doing?" Mom screamed at us. "I told you to come to Mommy's house, not over here."

I found myself with a mouthful of food again, unable to muster up anything besides "What are you talking about?"

"Margie," Jack said. "Calm down."

"Get out of my face," Mom yelled, pushing him away. There was no calming her down. In this family, when push came to shove, it was always better to opt for a stranglehold. Mom went for the jugular, but Jack held her back.

"Let go of me!" she screamed, and writhed free. My sister reached for a chip, enjoying the show. My mother plucked it out of her hand as if pulling the pin from a grenade, shaking, her eyes glazed over. I'd once gone running down a dirt road in the sticks outside of Orlando by myself, back in college, when a loose pit bull came hauling ass at me across its yard, barking and snarling a foot away, threatening to attack. I'd stopped running and put my hands down and slowly backed away from it. I had somehow calmed the dog. I did the same now, dropping my feta cheese, hands in the air, whispering, *It's okay, it's okay*, but that was not happening now. My mother was not backing down.

"I told you girls to come to Mommy's house," she yelled. "Not here. This is not where I said to go."

"We thought this is where the food was."

"Don't give me that. I told you to go to Mommy's."

"What does it matter?" I said.

"It matters because that's what I said to do. I'm your mother and you listen to me, not these people."

"Margie, calm down," Jack's wife, Susan, said.

"Don't tell me to calm down, you bitch."

"Don't talk to my mom like that," Beth said, and there was some heavy pushing now, some heavy shoving. My sister bolted to the car, and I took off running behind her.

"I told you to go to Grandma's house!" Mom came outside and screamed, as if we hadn't already heard her. "That's what I said!"

"We didn't know," we pleaded, but my mother kept right on screaming.

She didn't shut up until Molly threw the first punch, not at my mom, but right to her own face, hitting herself square in the forehead.

"What are you doing?" I said, almost laughing. "Stop."

My sister wouldn't stop though; she punched herself again, and then the car, and the dashboard and the windshield, laughing wildly. I feared she might get all *Heathers* with the cigarette jack. I curled up in my seat, but Mom naturally thrust herself into the middle of the mosh-pit-for-one. "Stop it. Stop doing that, goddamn it."

Mom reached her body into the car window to subdue my sister, but she couldn't, and my sister slapped her hard across the face. I knew what was coming next. I braced myself as my mother recoiled. Then she struck Molly so hard across the face, the streetlight went out.

We were driving nowhere then. We didn't go back home, not immediately. We drove around like in the glory days, going no place in particular. We switched seats and I drove us around Orange Lake. There wasn't much to see except the Christmas-card squirrel. Nothing much to say, so we didn't talk. *It takes a little time of getting used to,* we sang along with the Raveonettes, *but love can destroy everything.* We smoked a pack of cigarettes, stopped and had a beer at a crappy sports bar on Highway 19. When we got back to the house on Missouri Avenue it was after midnight, but Mom was waiting on a couch for us, sandwiched between a box of photo albums and a stack of cookbooks, snotty Kleenex scattered all around her like a field of tissue flowers.

"You betrayed me," she said.

"You're a psycho," Molly said, and tried to head to the Florida room.

"Oh, no you don't," Mom said. "You sit down. We're going to have a talk."

"Can I smoke first?" Molly said.

"Sit down," Mom yelled. "I'll just say this. If you talk to those people ever again—"

"To our family?" I asked.

"If you associate with those people ever again, I don't want anything to do with you. I already don't really want much to do with you right now."

I didn't understand her. I couldn't imagine why she'd been so hurt by her brother and sister, by Molly and me. We had no bad intentions in mind, but my dear mother in her orange kimono and towel turban like a living soft-serve ice cream, she just stared at us as if we were Grinches who'd just taken away her Who hash. She lectured us for an hour on what it means to be family, on how her relatives were all out to screw her over like a bunch of evil old farts in some *Scooby-Doo* episode. This was the only approach to suffering that she knew: martyr or nothing.

"You kids don't understand," she said. "It's my mother who's gone. You can't understand what it feels like."

If a funeral is a celebration of life, then this was no funeral. Uncle Jack arrived with the shotgun in his truck, and Aunt Susie didn't even show, having gone back north to turn herself in to Cross City Correctional. My mother drove separately from Molly and me, giving us the silent treatment. She didn't save us a seat. She didn't look at us, hug us, acknowledge us.

As if taking the witness stand, my sister read a short written statement in front of the chapel about how headstrong and stubborn my grandma was, but also how loving and forgiving, and how everyone needed to remember that the apple didn't fall far from the tree. It was an intriguing sentiment, if not exactly accurate. I'd only ever seen spoiled, rotten oranges fall from the trees around Grandma's house anyways.

After the service, some older relatives were holding a barbecue, so everybody went back to the house on Missouri Avenue to change into comfortable clothes before heading over. I put on a tank top and jeans.

"Is this okay to wear?" I asked Mom in the hall before she left.

If I lifted my arms over my head, you'd be able to see an inch of belly, but I didn't plan to carry any giant baskets of fruit up there all afternoon, exposing my midriff.

"I don't know," Mom said, exasperated. "If you want to look like a slut."

These were the only words she would speak to me for a month.

I went back to school. Christmas came and went. I exchanged mix tapes and CDs with my friends, lay in my bathtub all winter drowning myself in Built to Spill albums, smoked Winstons, played pool, fixed up the guitar Aunt Susie gave me, studied Faulkner, fucked off like my mother told me to. Then one day I finally got a phone call from her.

"I just wanted you to know that I forgive you and Molly," she said. "We're family and we gotta stick together."

"Okay," I said. I bit my lip. I didn't give her a piece of my mind. I didn't say, *How dare you take your mother's death out on us. How dare you be so selfish.* Not then, not ever.

"How are you doing?" I asked. "I miss you." I really did.

"Well, I got fired from my job. They said I was being pushy. Can you believe that?"

She told me about how the young people at her job had banded together against her so-called bad attitude, and I told her about how the young people at my school had so-called bands.

"I met this one chick who also plays guitar," I said. "We're thinking of starting a folk-duo type thing. There's a cool little music scene going on here."

"Honey," she said, interrupting me, dead serious. "Are you a lesbian?"

"No."

"Because sometimes I just get the feeling that you may be a lesbian, and there's nothing wrong with that. I still love you."

"Mom," I said. "I'm not a lesbian." I wondered what she was doing right now, if she was lying on Molly's old bed in her mother's old nightgown, surrounded by magazines and folded laundry and tchotchkes and dust bunnies that flittered around like little storm clouds all over the boxes on the floor. It made me anxious to picture the insanity of it all, but I took the first steps I could toward helping her, and myself, feel better. I said, "I still love you too."

Christmas with Homos

G one were the days of Christmas at Grandma's with her illegally chopped-down Christmas tree and a dozen twelve-packs of beer from Sam's Club, wrapped and awaiting random cousins and hunting buddies who always showed up unannounced. Since my grandma had passed away, Mom was on speaking terms with one person in the family, so there was only this option: Aunt Libby would visit the house with sugar-free desserts, towel turbans, and Humane Society calendars, inquiring about relationship and fertility status. This year we'd also been signed on to attend a Christmas Eve candle-lighting service.

I already knew the phone call that had transpired, Mom telling her, "Wendy's bringing a friend home."

"A boyfriend?"

"No. A girl. They have a folk duo up in North Carolina."

"Oh."

This friend was Xhenet. She knew nothing about how loud it was possible for my mother to scream when angered, but having a stranger around ensured Mom would be on her best behavior. In the history of her psycho tics, my mother usually had to know one of my friends at least a full two weeks to feel comfortable going full Bitch Treatment in front of them, and we were going to stay for only four days. Plus, Xhenet was not at all the type of person my family would want to yell in front of or directly at. Her brother had recently passed away, so she'd already been home to Connecticut and wasn't planning to go back for Christmas. She was friendly and smart. Better still, she was an Albanian and a vegetarian, so we'd all have something to talk about.

"I made baklava," she said, holding up a Saran-wrapped plate of something very soggy as we loaded the car.

"What's wrong with it?"

"I think it just needs to sit for a while."

The baklava sat for twelve hours and looked the same when we arrived at the house on Missouri Avenue. We stood on a snowman doormat stacked on a plastic-grass doormat on top of a brown carpet on top of the cold hard cement, and rang the doorbell.

"It doesn't work anymore!" Mom screamed from inside. "Is that you? Hold on."

On top of an old sewing-machine table, a giant glass ashtray held a blooming onion of butts, a sign my sister had already been here and already escaped. I hadn't stepped foot in the house in a year, but if the porch was any indication, things were not good. I'd prepped Xhenet about the extent of the clutter, but still her eyes seemed ridden with a resounding *Jesus*. One table exploded with poinsettias, another with pinecones and gulf sponges. A tall metal lamp with eight bendable octopus arms lurked in a corner, where an old wooden rocking chair sat with its seat blown out as if the former occupant just up and exploded right there, taking one of the porch screens with him.

The door swung open, and we screamed as a dead body in a garbage bag fell at our feet.

"Did you finally kill John?" I asked as Mom lifted it back up.

"It's just fabric," she said. "Lay off, why don't you?"

John was in his La-Z-Boy, seemingly dead until Xhenet announced, "I made baklava."

Then he was up on his toes with Sheldon the cat. They were practically one and the same, both getting fatter and grayer with each passing year, waking only to eat, use the restroom, and run from my mother when she yelled at them to stop nosing around her things. Give them a newspaper and they were interested one minute, asleep the next. Bring a treat in the house, and they circled like buzzards.

"What's baklava?" John asked, examining the foreign matter.

"Damn it, John," Mom said. "You've had baklava before."

"I've never had this type of baklava."

Xhenet and I sat on a new couch—a new *used* couch. It was a beige couch from John's uncle Dale, the only one of three you could sit on without crushing something of minor importance, but it was a sinker. It swallowed us up, and suddenly we were eye level with dozens of presents piled on the floor.

"Are those beers from Sam's Club?" I asked.

"Well, I didn't know who was going to stop by," Mom said, which meant Xhenet would be getting a twelve-pack or two for Christmas. Afghans and throw pillows dumped on our heads as we were drawn deeper into the couch's ass cheeks.

"Comfy, huh?" Mom asked. "Well, excuse the junk."

She'd always said this to any new person who so dared enter her lair. She sat back in a chair and pretended not to be lodged inside the Christmas tree. "We're trying to deal with it. We just moved the other couch to the garage."

"There was another couch?" I asked. "In here?"

"What's this called again?" John asked, fiddling with the Saran wrap. "Baklava?"

"Don't open that in here," Mom scolded him. "Go put it in the kitchen."

I noticed it for the first time then. Mom was doing something bizarre with her hand on her head. She was scratching her scalp, picking at it unnaturally, some type of new agitation.

"And don't make a goddamn mess in there," she yelled at John. She rolled her eyes, scratching and scratching. "He's all whacked-out on meds."

He'd picked up something called the Dan Dee dancing Christmas chicken at CVS, another impulse buy on a long list of frivolous animatronic purchases. "Lookit," he said now, pressing a button. The chicken did its chicken dance on the dining table, dangerously close to knocking over a dozen porcelain animals fleeing a manger.

"Stop playing that damn chicken on the table," Mom said. "I told you before."

So John moved it to the floor, where the chicken did its dance into the side of a trunk of Christmas junk and landed face-first, flailing on the ground, still attempting to move. Sometimes it's impossible to break your ugly habits, even when it means hurting yourself.

"Mom," I asked, "what's with the scalp?"

"Oh, sorry," she said. "It's just been itching me lately. I don't know if it's a rash or what."

She smoothed her hair in place and quickly changed the subject. "How about we bring those suitcases in and get you girls settled?"

One time, back in high school, I went spelunking with my cross-country team at the Lost Sea Adventure caverns up in Tennessee and there were very small crevices we had to wedge ourselves into, sometimes in absolute darkness. *Y'all go slow,* the guide had said in his drawl, warning us that a jaguar had plunged to its death here back in prehistoric times. None of that prepared me for entry to my own bedroom with the lights on.

"I've been trying to clear this out so we can fit the suitcases," Mom said, but the door could barely open, plagued by an over-the-door wardrobe rack of Grandma's blouses and business suits.

"Here, hold these," she said, handing me a stack of clothes so she could get the door open without knocking over a stalagmite of shoe boxes.

"What are all these?"

"Some shoes I got." She'd inherited a few thousand dollars after Grandma passed and was managing to spend it all at T.J.Maxx from the looks of it. "I have nowhere to put them right now until I rearrange that closet."

"Which closet?"

"Well, a couple closets. Cool it, why don't you?"

My bed was covered in ugly plastic flower art in the hot-doggish colors of the 1970s, and on top was the scary baby doll of Mom's youth, one of its arms torn off and resting nearby.

"What happened to your doll?"

"Oh, it's horrible isn't it? I was trying to rearrange some books on the shelf and she fell off."

"You can probably fix the arm."

"I know. I just haven't had time. I want to get this room cleared out, so I can fit my desk and sewing machine in here. Then I can use it as my office."

It was just that there was a mountain of junk, a sea of junk, a world of junk keeping that from happening. I felt the weight of it, the burden of it, bearing down on me, crushing me. I couldn't even relax after a full day on the road. There wasn't enough room for two carry-on-sized bags in here.

"It's just three more days," Xhenet said encouragingly. I felt bad then. Maybe I'd made a mistake asking her to come home with me for the holiday. I thought it would help perk her up, help perk my mom up. But I could see the whole four days would teeter like the tall stacks of Mom's *Utne Reader*s under the air-conditioning vent. Xhenet wedged herself into the sinker couch like a *Double Dare* finalist and slept, but I couldn't bring myself to.

It wasn't just three more days. Imagine your mother burying herself alive. Imagine knowing there's nothing you can do to help her. Imagine this every day of your life.

Later, I heard my sister pull up and come inside. She slid open the door to her room, a sound I remembered well, and then went to the bathroom, the thin wall separating her from my head. She took a shower and went to the kitchen, opening the fridge. I got up to see her, no easy feat in the dark.

"Hey," I said.

"Hey."

We stood there and shook our heads for a long time, just looking around. Kind of chuckling, our eyes permanently rolling. But deep down I was frightened. I was terrified and annoyed. My mother had already gotten a second storage space for fabric alone, and that wasn't counting the garage. She'd turned our home into an antiques mall, the kind that borders on junk shop, the kind you must contort your body to walk through or else you'll get charged for breaking something. And you'll always get charged for breaking something. This was our fate, our problem, our relationship being chipped away at one broken poodle figurine at a time.

"Have you seen my room?" I asked.

"Have you seen *my* room?" Molly asked.

I poked my head in and there were boxes all over. Junk all over. Christmas things and sewing things and fabric and patterns and lord knows what other things. You couldn't even see what used to be in this room, except for those same goddamn frilly white sheers that had always been around peeking out from behind everything like a petticoat.

"Oh god," I said. "This is fucking bad."

"I don't want to talk about it."

She never did. She just walled herself off whenever shit got bad, always had.

❧

The next morning, Mom heard Xhenet and me messing around in my old room with the door closed and was on us immediately. "What are you doing in there?"

"Nothing."

She barged right in, busting us in the midst of throwing out old CD jewel cases. "Oh, you should go through those and pick out the good ones."

"There's no CDs in them. They're just cases. We can toss them."

"But they're perfectly good cases."

"Are you really that attached to Carnie Wilson?" I asked. "I mean, what is going on in here?"

"I'm trying to get a handle on it, okay?" she said. "Now lay off." And since it was the second time she'd told me to lay off since coming home, I did. If she had to say it a third time, an ax-wielding Bloody Mary might very well appear in one of the fifteen cracked mirrors leaned up against the wall.

"I'll take a jewel case," Xhenet said. "The one with Mick Fleetwood on it."

"That's the spirit," I said.

To celebrate, Mom took us all to Chili's.

What fun we were having now. We ate our spinach-artichoke dip. We looked for shoes at Ross Dress for Less and stood in line at Target, because that's what Mom wanted to do, purchase more presents and wrapping paper two days before Christmas.

"I'll be outside smoking," Molly said. Here was a person who had long understood one of life's greatest secrets: find something you love to do and always make time for it.

Back at the house, we settled in for some afternoon Lifetime network and wrapping presents. Each item Mom put under the tree was marked for *Xhenet* and *Xhenet* and *Xhenet* again. We weren't going to bring up her deceased brother, but if the topic arose, Mom had already purchased enough microfleece socks for Xhenet to feel comfort and joy for the next ten years. Things were going fine until Molly stole away with the phone and asked Mom what time we'd be eating dinner.

"I don't know. Why?"

"Because I'm trying to figure out when I can meet up with Sherry. We're going to get drinks tonight."

"Oh."

"Do you really not want me to meet my friends out?"

"Do what you want," Mom said, but she didn't mean it. "I guess I'll start dinner."

"Start it when you want," Molly said. "I guess I'm staying in."

"Go out and party if that's what you want to do. God forbid you spend some time with your family."

Molly hadn't yet mastered the art of Aunt Susie, who partied in front of the family but simply locked herself in a bedroom when she needed the hard stuff. Mom went to the kitchen, slamming pans and chopping vegetables as if the counter were covered in poisonous snakes.

"Mom," I said, rather worried. "Do you need some help?"

"No. You kids don't care about what I want. You all act like this is so horrible."

I called in the Albanian for backup.

"I can help," Xhenet offered.

"Xhenet loves to cook, Mom. Did you try the baklava?"

At the sound of it, John and Sheldon rose from their afternoon slumber, hovering near the entry to the kitchen.

"I'm hungry, Margie," John groaned.

"Don't come in here!" Mom screamed, teetering on madness.

"Why don't you let us make some snacks?" I asked.

She had easily hacked celery and carrots into snack size already. We pulled out some cheese, dips, and fruit. Mostly they just fell out of the fridge when we opened the door. It was that easy. Suddenly we had snacks. We weren't at Chili's, but we were close.

On Christmas Eve, Mom selected Molly to retrieve Aunt Libby from her retirement community, a sure sign she wanted Molly to suffer the punishment of Britches's tear gas for hauling us to get drinks with Sherry in Tampa the night before. Aunt Libby could no longer drive at night, just as she could no longer detect the foul odor that emanated from her pet, her senses weakening in older age except when it came to taste in male movie stars: the oilier the abs, the better.

"Well looky here," she said the second she entered the house, the body bag pitching into the doorway behind her. "Just look at all these beautiful presents."

The living room appeared to be covered in a sparkly yuletide fungus. It had spread over the magazines, trunks, vases, baskets, and bookshelves. I don't want to brag, but when you have a selection of vintage wrapping papers, bows, ribbons, and tags that are carefully folded and saved every Christmas for three decades, you have a lot of options to dazzle the elderly.

"Here, sit down," we told Aunt Libby, putting her half-inside the tree.

"Margie, you wouldn't believe it," Aunt Libby said. "I went over to Jack's last night and Beth is pregnant."

"Pregnant?" Mom asked from the kitchen, jabbing tiny spears of clove into the ham.

"Yes, apparently her and Jim have been trying for a while, so Jack can have him some grandbabies. But anyways, they got me a laptop for Christmas. Can you believe it? A laptop. I about died of a heart attack."

"A laptop," Mom said, walking out from the kitchen. Her smile was so big and flimsy you could only walk halfway across it before the thing snapped in two. "How very nice of them."

"Now, don't let that make you feel bad. I don't have money to throw around like that, and I know you don't either, what with losing your job and all. I don't expect nothing like that from y'all."

"Well, good," Mom said. " 'Cause we sure as shit can't afford that."

"Now, Margie. You know I'm fine with whatever I get. Jack had a good tax season this year. They just went and got a new boat too."

"How nice for them," Mom said.

"Well, should we open presents now or after the service?" Aunt Libby said, sweat pouring off her face. The vintage bubble lights had finally heated up, so hot they were warping nearby ornaments.

The handful of women at Aunt Libby's church were a little too close to death to be called the Sunshine Choir. There were five of them, tiny, frail things with poufy hair like the tops of cartoon trees you draw when you're in grade school, greeting us on the way in with their cold, gummy hands. Aunt Libby was sort of a celebrity at the church, an old-timer who ran the West Pasco Methodist Women's Club and had been around long enough to lean over and say things like, "You know they have all kinds of poor folks coming in here now. I don't mind, but you know, they only come because of the free supper. We get a lot of homeless lining up outside. You'll see."

The service began when the Sunshine Choir took the stage and shrieked, "Hark! The Herald . . . ," as if being burned alive in their long white polyester robes. They warbled the classic noel, the unintelligible Christmas carol, the comfort and joy trumped by impossible dreams, angels high on medication. The congregation sang along with notes nobody could hit without applying their Beaker impersonation.

The conductor of the Sunshine Choir was a man in his late sixties or early seventies, a whippersnapper compared to the prosthetic hips in the alto section. He directed them with baton in hand, his arms thrashing like those of a drowning victim. When "peace on earth" almost got a soprano another eye patch, my mother looked past Aunt Libby and Xhenet, and down at my sister and me, smiling. I smiled back, striking up in the Beaker range, while a gigantic woman in the pew before me turned around with the evil eye.

I didn't care. It had been a long time since I'd seen my mother happy, so I continued to sing proudly with the deformed Santa pin of my childhood clamped to my chest. The Sunshine Choir carried on for another half hour, finally stopping for the pastor, who read various passages from the Bible I had never learned. Sunday mornings, for us, had always been a time to mindlessly watch Richard Simmons and Susan Powter infomercials and eat Toaster Strudel in bed. In adulthood, I'd come to realize that's called a hangover.

Finally the fluorescent lights dimmed; after an interlude of high-pitched feedback from the preacher's microphone headset, he soothingly informed us that the candle-lighting ceremony would now get under way.

"And please, everyone, stand and help me welcome to the stage Mrs. Lauretta Homo."

Homo. It was there in the program: *Holiday Methodist would like to thank the Homo family for their help on Christmas Eve 2004.*

This Homo was onstage now in her crisp red sweater set and tan polyester pants, her hair a poufy cloud of kindergarten tree. The pastor lit her Christmas candle and she was off, setting the other Homos aflame. Suddenly, Homo kids, Homo grandkids, and little newborn Homos poured out of the front two pews with their shiny metal trays and lit candles. Homo grandpas and Homo uncles. Homo cousins and Homo stepsons. The Homos were among us, handing over the money trays, collecting the trays on the other side.

Then they fell in, and we all stood, the entire flaming congregation. The lights were turned off. Small creatures were released from a crate somewhere off in the distance. It was the Sunshine Choir, finding their way back onstage in the candlelight. The big screen turned black and showed a NO DATA message in the red and green colors of the holiday while "Silent Night" rang out on the organ. By the second verse, the Sunshine Choir was lost, unable to read in the dim light, and everyone hummed instead. It was the sound of peace on earth. Then somebody opened the back door and a long stream of glowing white light descended upon those of us in the back rows. I turned to see him there, a single homeless Jesus peeking his head in the door of the chapel.

He didn't step inside but stayed in the lobby, looking around for a minute before a Homo closed the door on him. I saw the other homeless folks outside the main door of the church then too, smoking cigarettes and hunched over in the rare Florida cold, waiting to be let in for supper.

"Merry Christmas," one told us on the way out, and my

mother, out of nowhere, drew a twenty-dollar bill from her purse and placed it in his hand.

"Thank you," he said. "You're a kind lady."

"You didn't have to do that, Margie," Libby said when we got back in the car. "You never know if they're going to spend it on crack or whatever it is they smoke these days."

"It's Christmas for Christ's sake," Mom said.

She drove us through Holiday and on back home to New Port Richey, where we'd open our Humane Society calendars and model our new towel turbans for the camera. This year, when Aunt Libby asked if we wanted the sugarless pecan pie or the sugarless brownies, we'd all try at least one, telling her how delicious they were.

"You don't have to eat it," she'd say.

But we would. We all would. Every bite so sweet it hurt.

II.

Nut Treasures

When You Board the Party Bus

I'd been living on Molly's futon for two whole days when I landed my first job in New Orleans at Tales of the Cocktail. This is the largest conference and trade show for the spirits and bartending industry in the world, right during July, the sweatiest pig of months. I wasn't qualified in any way to work with so much booze at one time. I'd stayed away from frou-frou cocktails since my sister brought me to a crappy French Quarter restaurant back during a Halloween trip in 2003. I'd ordered a Pink Squirrel and received a martini glass of Pepto-Bismol. I'd spent the next four years washing that taste away with Mickey's Big Mouths in North Carolina's finest dive bars and still considered vodka something to be chugged warm from the bottle at a house party while friends set fire to the bathroom trash can or went to the ER with an arm sliced open by a machete.

Tales of the Cocktail didn't know that. They didn't know

anything about me. I simply e-mailed my résumé and got hired two hours later. There was no interview, phone call, or meeting to discuss my useless college degrees, my worthless skills, my ability to recite the first stanza of "Der Erlkönig" from memory, or the fact that I was currently homeless, unemployed, and watching my sister's cat pee on my suitcase again. There was just an e-mail instructing me to show up at a storage facility at seven the next morning if I wanted a job, so I did.

I was there to help repack swag bags, a supervisor informed me. A swag bag is a bag filled with free products for people who don't need free products. It's a pack rat's dream, just lots of stuff nobody asked for piled on more stuff nobody needs, presented as a little welcome gift for existing.

"But some things got broken," the supervisor said, unlocking three large storage spaces. Before us sat two hundred bags of what celebrity vodka brand owner Dan Aykroyd might have described as Bags O'Glass. We needed to go through every single bag and repack them.

"It's kind of a nightmare," the supervisor said, but *kind of a nightmare* pretty much defined my recent work history. I'd spent a year grading standardized-test essays written by America's worst fifth and eleventh graders, seated at a brown folding table in a subarctic strip mall. Before that, I'd baked and bagged cookies in a factory where we weren't allowed to sit down and the bosses let their children and black Lab run around unsupervised until streaks of smeared feces appeared all over the employee bathroom one day.

A sea of green Whole Foods bags filled with free booze seemed a tropical island away from all that. I quickly went to work, impressing interns in sorority shirts with my ability to unpack and discard things at lightning speed. Repacking swag is hard work, but I owned this job. All over the hallways, I organized airplane bottles of sake, vodka, and sake vodka. I sorted and stacked. I parceled out muddlers that evoked every type of sex toy and things that just sounded like sex toys: jiggers, shakers, swizzle sticks, can openers, and juicers.

"Feel free to take any extra product home," the supervisor informed me at the end of the day.

As I dumped fifths of whiskey all over my sister's dining table that night, she danced around in her new Absolut aviator sunglasses and Malibu bandana like some belligerent Axl Rose, squealing, "This is the best job you've ever had."

At first it did seem that way. I'd always considered the salad-dressing-prep position I'd held down for years at a low-country restaurant my best job ever, mainly because I didn't have to deal with humans, only the subhumans who worked back of house and continually drew penises on the 86 board. Now I'd done such a good job with the swag that I'd been hired on as a room supervisor. The conference was at the Hotel Monteleone, known for its ornate rotating Carousel Bar, gleaming marble halls, and old-fartish carpeting, the type you'd expect *Designing Women* was rolled up in when they hauled it off of the CBS soundstage. Here there were no subhumans, or regular humans, but mixologists, brand ambassadors, and food writers. Everything was created to accommodate. There was a third-wave coffee stand and a smoothie bar. A team of kiwifruit salespeople wandered around offering halves of kiwifruit with sporks stuck in them. In the staff home base, where trays of sandwiches and cheese sat untouched, I was encouraged by my own supervisors to take breaks and sit down whenever necessary, to try the cocktails and have some fun.

Have some fun was what my former manager at an Irish pub said whenever he wanted me to flirt with guys who ordered pitchers of green beer while plates of shepherd's pie melted the skin off my palms. I'd never been the type to associate work with pleasure but more with urgent care and desperation. I was pacing nervously in my gaudy seminar room, unsure what I was doing at all, when a human pineapple poked his head in, holding out a tiki drink.

"Oh my god," he said. "Try this."

I had no idea who this spiky-haired person was. Still, he handed me a concoction and urged me to take a sip. "It's just a little Scorpion Bowl. They're handing them out in the lobby. They set it on fire and everything. Go get one."

Days before, I'd come to New Orleans thinking I wouldn't drink excessively or smoke cigarettes or party too much. I'd get an okay job and an apartment, keep trudging along in my sister's shadow, as I'd always felt comfortable doing. But here it was, my fourth day in town, and somebody was already setting my drink on fire at eight thirty in the morning. At work. Tales of the Cocktail likely knew this would happen, which is why I'd been strapped into a walkie-talkie headset that barked orders on channel E, telling me my first seminar started in thirty minutes: *Sending over volunteers now.*

A seasoned vet of all the previous Tales, Deb, arrived in her pink neon scrunchie and Stein Mart sandals with glazed doughnuts for everyone. I shoved three in my face, hoping to sober up.

"This is your first year, I can tell," she said. "I volunteer for everything. Jazz Fest. French Quarter Fest. The thing about Tales is you really have to pace yourself. It's a marathon, honey, not a sprint."

This, I'd come to learn, is something New Orleanians love to tell newcomers about any event where at least one person in the crowd is bound to die from alcohol poisoning while dressed in their wife's lingerie. My second volunteer, Betty, on the other hand, was fresh off the boat like me. She told us that she was just passing through New Orleans this summer and was volunteering because she had nothing better to do. With her stained capris, worn tennis shoes, and cigarette-stained skin, she reminded me of the women I'd worked with back at the cookie factory—ladies who lived in trailers and played cards on the weekends, their bottle-blond hair long hardened by the stinging White Rain of life. Every single one of them had been sweet as day-old pastry. *Make us proud*, they told me the day I quit and headed across town to grade illegible standardized essays. Little did they know I'd be eating cheese cubes out of a wadded napkin at a booze conference someday.

"Where ya from, dawlin'?" Deb asked me.

"North Carolina, by way of Florida."

"What brings you to New Orleans?"

Desperation. Fear. Having nowhere else to go, unless I wanted to move back in with my mother like some thousands of other unemployed twentysomethings with horrendous student loan debt. "My sister lives here," I told her, "and I wanted to move somewhere cool after graduate school."

"Well, you'll fit right in," she said. "I can tell."

We lugged in a day's worth of alcohol from a hall closet as big as a liquor store. The single task made me sweat through my shirt, which was good. I was sobering up a bit when the enabling pineapple poked his head back in, carrying a tray of tiny clear shots.

"We have to do a good-luck toast," he said, handing us drinks. He poked his head in after the first seminar and the second, doling out the shots.

"I'm Miguel, by the way," he said, finally introducing himself by the end of the day. "And I'm so getting laid this week. Here's to getting laid."

"Here's to getting laid," we said.

Though all I could think about was getting to lie down on my sister's futon and sleeping for a solid thirteen hours, or however long it took for the spins to go away.

It was impossible to sleep that long at Molly's house, however. Each morning she rose at six to drink coffee and read the paper while cigarette smoke poured from the kitchen, before heading off to work at a library in a medical science center. Then she'd return home at 6:00 P.M. to her personal smog. She was in the kitchen, putting together a salad for us Peg Bundy style, when I wandered in, slimy stains on my shirt and jeans.

"Ew. What happened to you?"

"Some bartender tried to teach me how to shake a drink, and it exploded all over me."

"How's it going other than that?"

"Oh, fine," I said.

But it wasn't fine, not really. Everyone at Tales of the Cocktail had expensive outfits and smartphones and spoke about cocktails as if they belonged to a religious cult. "They all have cards and brands and stuff. I just feel like a loser, you know?"

"Well, you can get cards made at Kinko's. Oh, by the way, I revised your résumé and printed out fifty copies for you. You're welcome."

My sister had been saving my butt for years. She'd paid for various trips to Coachella, Suwannee Springfest, New Orleans, and the beach. When she was in college, she used to come down and rescue me from Mom's house. The year after Molly left, Mom had fallen asleep at the wheel and flipped John's Blazer, the only nice car he ever had, on the way home from an architecture ball. Naturally, she'd stayed bedridden for months longer than she needed to, letting me serve her, building a cage of magazines and knickknacks around the bed until she looked trapped in the middle of the room, like Hannibal before he gouges a pen into a guard's throat. Molly snuck me Manic Panic to dye my hair pink and introduced me to the Descendents. She took me to punk shows at the State Theatre in St. Pete. She took me to my first college party, where stoners watched midget porn. We weren't like Mom and Susie, who at seven years apart seemed relative strangers. Molly, for me, was an extension of myself, albeit a nerdier and more successful one. I'd never done much for her, had no resources to. She'd stayed at my house for a few days after Katrina hit but ended up going to house-sit in Philadelphia after some guy in a bar made fun of her tattoo, a single word, *mouse*, from Shelley Jackson's *Skin* project.

"If I ever make it big," I promised her now, "I'll buy you all kinds of furs."

"It's fine," she said. "I think Mr. Go might have peed on the futon while we were gone."

~

By the next day, *Kiwi? Kiwi? Kiwi? Kiwi?* poured in from the halls as if the big white spork population of New Zealand resided just beyond the doors to my conference room. Attendees no longer made it to the seminars at nine in the morning. A few staggered drunkenly in the halls, having never gone to bed. When approached with kiwifruit, they ran toward the nearest bathroom or doorway as if avoiding psycho ex-girlfriends.

"Just take one, and enjoy it," a kiwi team member said, cornering a drunk guy in a Sailor Jerry hat, aiming a spork at his face.

The attendees who did make the seminars left slimy uneaten fruit and cocktails all over the tables. They spit into buckets and kicked their chairs over while stampeding out of the room.

I'd learned my lesson and paced myself when it came to the complimentary drinks, but Betty had not heeded the advice of the natives and downed every drink the human pineapple handed out. While bitters experts, social media people, and apple brandy scholars tried to discuss the ins and outs of the industry for audiences of gassy cattle in beads, Deb and I rolled her under the refreshments table for a nap and made small talk.

By the time our 4:00 P.M. Bloggers Party was about to start,

Deb practically knew my life story, telling the guy in charge, "Gwendolyn here is a writer."

"Oh, really?" he said.

"Trying to be," I said. "I've had a couple stories published."

"Perfect. Do you have a card?"

"I don't."

"Oh, well. Who have you written for?"

"Have you ever heard of *Quarterly West* or *Crazyhorse*?"

"I haven't," he said,

"They're literary magazines," I said.

He slowly backed away, avoiding me for the duration of the welcome party, while the bloggers crowded around celebrity guest Ted Allen from *Queer Eye* in their belted, avuncular jeans. Women from Southern media outlets wore hats so large they looked like cat beds with feather toys poking out the top and downed the complimentary rum punch and questionable onion dip. One of them attempted to pull a chair out and sit, landing fat-bottomed on the floor, a small Chihuahua flying from her enormous zebra-print purse.

Deb helped the disheveled woman up, but she shooed her away. "I'm fine, darling, fine," she huffed, loading the Chihuahua back into her bag and heading off to another soiree, draped over a friend whose wig had completely tilted on its axis.

The stated mission of Tales of the Cocktail happens to be "saving the cocktail," which, though it sounds unimportant to some of us, has more advocates than, say, saving an African wild dog or some poison-dart toad. While that's all nice, the conference is mainly just a means for booze brands to throw a barrage of insane nightly parties. There are parties with cows you can milk to make your own Ramos Gin Fizz, parties with burlesque dancers and unicorn ice-cube sculptures, mime midgets on stilts, and other things you'd expect if somebody handed an event planner $200,000 and said, *Make it look like Gatsby does hallucinogens and wakes up in a spaceship with King Tut, a case of vodka, and some monkeys that have just discovered they have nipples.*

"You should try to get us tickets to something," Molly had told me encouragingly earlier in the week. Not shocking, even though my sister and I had a history of failing to have fun in public ever since a frat boy showed us his pecker at a Millencolin show back in 1997. Something bad usually happened when two certified weirdo magnets hit the town. But it just so happened that on the last night, my supervisors handed me two wristbands to a closing event.

"This is so rad," my sister said, meeting me at the front gate of Mardi Gras World. There were chefs set up between massive carnival floats and bartenders making cocktails in fake saloons and speakeasies as people milled about in between showgirls walking live alligators on leashes.

"It's so nice to pretend I deserve to be here," I said.

"I know, right?" Molly said. "If another Gatsby gives me a dirty look, I'm going to start stabbing people with my high heels."

We downed plates of crawfish Monica and watched more drunk Gatsbys have a dance-off to "SexyBack." Nothing bad happened, but we still stood around deflating by the minute. Booze always had the same effect on both of us, making our ankles give out along with our self-worth. Despite having a perfect GPA in high school and college, an amazing job, model features, no financial worries, and an attractive big-time-engineer boyfriend, my sister suffered from relatively lower self-esteem than me—a broke, homeless, jobless human tethered to an island of student debt.

"That's it," Molly said, pointing to a pod of women in orca-slick party dresses. "Those girls just gave me a dirty look."

"No, they didn't," I said.

One of the girls stepped up. "Excuse me," she said. "Are you an instructor at LSU's medical school? Because we were just talking about how your research class was, like, the best one we've ever taken. It was so funny."

"Why, yes, that is me," my sister said, really hamming it up.

"You're an asshole," I told her after the students were gone. An asshole with a wreck of a sister, but we both had a French 75 in hand, and when a newspaper photographer approached us, we fluffed up our hair and posed like we were at senior prom.

A few weeks after Tales of the Cocktail, I got an e-mail from the events founder inviting all staff and volunteers out to the country for a barbecue. I'd already settled into a new job at a cheese shop uptown and had moved into a crappy apartment in the Lower Garden District, a few blocks from the infamous Walmart on Tchoupitoulas, where during Katrina pretty much everything but a couple Brooke Hogan CDs had been looted. It was the safest or most dangerous area in New Orleans, depending on how you felt about cop cars circling your block every moment of the night and day. There was a bunch of college missionary kids rebuilding a house next door, and one had a guitar, believing himself a real Jack Johnson. They gathered on the front porch every evening, singing endless praise songs. A trip to the country, however brief, sounded like a dream.

There were maybe a dozen people on the bus, including the human pineapple and Betty. I brought along my sister and her boyfriend, Chris.

Before you ever agree to ride a party bus heading an hour and a half out into the Louisiana sticks though, let me tell you this: Always make sure there is a bathroom on board. The ride out to the country was not the problem. It was fine. The party itself was lovely. There were bales of hay and picnic tables and the sun set on the huge green lawn and on past the cypress trees and bayou. The problem was the limoncello. A bartender was set up in a barn with his homemade variation of a lemon drop, which went down like nectar. By the time the bus was being boarded back to New Orleans, folks were stumbling all over the place. The human pineapple was lifting up women's dresses during photos, he was so inebriated. As we loaded the bus to return, there were twice as many people aboard. We waved good-bye to the estate, which now looked like a car lot. Designated drivers who'd promised to drive home had abandoned their vehicles, promising to return at first light, knowing full well they wouldn't be able to rise from bed until two days later.

We'd been on the back roads for thirty minutes when the driver got a concerned look in his eye and consulted those of us in the first two rows. He'd taken a wrong turn somewhere on a back road, and we were now lost in the dark of night. Every time he backtracked, every turn he made, got us deeper into coon-ass country. There were no gas stations. No fast-food joints or streetlights. By hour two, there was only loud farting and screaming due to the barbecue now being digested, and brains that had long since given up on coherent sentence formation.

"I me trash cat," a girl in back yelled at her boyfriend. "Trash cat. I me trash cat."

When he ran to the front and retrieved the trash can, the driver didn't even stop him.

By the time we found the interstate, almost everyone had passed out. And then the scent came. Betty, sprawled out across the aisle from Molly and Chris, had managed to both piss and shit her khaki capris in her sleep. I covered my face with a napkin, listening to a guy in madras shorts snore across the aisle from me, until at three in the morning, we were finally dropped off in the Dorignac's grocery store parking lot in Metairie. People fled immediately. We were about to leave when I noticed Betty had stumbled off the bus and was leaning against a light post in the parking lot, with no intention of moving.

"Do you need a ride home?" I asked her, and she shrugged. "Where do you live?"

"Canal," she mumbled, along with something that vaguely resembled, "I love Dinah Shore."

"Do you have a license or ID on you?"

She pushed her tan purse at me, and I dug around, found her license. It was a unlaminated Colorado ID from a different era, one in which Betty still wore the Farrah Fawcett hairdo of better days but had started taking makeup cues from Boy George. By now, everybody had left the parking lot, including the bus driver. She had no cash for a cab. She could barely stand. We did what we needed to: loaded her into the truck bed like a bag of sod, telling her not to sit up.

Chris had just merged onto I-10 when Betty sat up, pressing her face into the glass and scaring the living shit out of me. "Lay down!" I screamed, and she obeyed. I opened the back window when we hit Canal and she propped herself up again, perusing the street like she'd never seen it before. She nodded off a little to the left, which I took to mean we should turn left, so we looped around to Carrollton. This whole section of Mid-City had sat underwater after Katrina, and now, not even two years later, most of the houses were under construction, trailers in front yards, debris piled on the side of the road. That was the summer the power kept going out any time you blinked, and it had gone out now. Everything was pitch-black, even the streetlights out.

Betty told us to stop. We helped her out of the back and into a yard, where she stumbled and went face-first into the front steps of a FEMA trailer. She got to her knees and mumbled something. "Just go," she was saying, "just go." We could've called the cops or knocked on the door, but we didn't do either. We got back in the truck and pulled away.

People always say there's something so magical about when you first move to New Orleans, about how different it is from any other place, how special and cultural. In many ways, I suppose that's true. Your first Parkway po' boy, say, or the first time a high school marching band comes up the street to practice out of nowhere. But staring out the back window at Betty in her soiled clothes in the dim moonlight, I could only see the romantic notion of New Orleans for what it really was: falling face-first onto somebody else's lawn.

A Round of Applause from the Completely Unhinged

Like many classically trained artists before him, Robin didn't like to bathe. The closest he came to a daily shower was rinsing undershirts in the sink, hanging them over the back porch to dry so that dirt lines eventually covered the thin white material in a sort of hobo plaid. If you've never dated a hobo, you can certainly ease into it by going out with a person who finds discarded work pants on the sidewalk and squeals with delight. We'd first met on lower Decatur, the only two people dancing to Miami Sound Machine in a club at two in the morning, so I didn't have any grandiose ideas about him. He could have amazing hour-long discussions on Camus and Derrida, but turn the conversation to something as simple as hand washing or a hair comb and you'd lost him forever.

Still, I thought him mysterious. A few weeks after we met, Robin took my hand as we sat together drinking beers on his stoop and without any irony at all said, "I've done a lot of disturbing things in my life."

"Well, geez," I probed. "Like what?"

"Just things that would really disturb you."

Well into his thirties, Robin still owned a beanbag chair. Hardly anything on earth seemed more disturbing than that. He drove a Chevy, the sexiest kind, old and rusty. Brittle seats, dirty ashtray, only started when you popped the hood and connected the battery cables yourself, with obligatory cigarette in mouth and dog whining in the front seat.

"My truck's all messed up," he told me the first time I rode shotgun.

"It's not that bad," I said as makeup melted down my face and neck, pooling between my boobs like a wad of Silly Putty in the heat.

"Sure. I'll just be the guy with the truck that won't start and the windows that won't roll down."

"No you won't," I told him, and I was being totally honest.

That was all before he gave me a staph infection.

It's just a bite, I told myself when the red welt first appeared. Apparently a lot of people do this, mistaking their infection for the mark of an ant or insect, some spider that danced offstage in a top hat and white gloves before you realized it'd done a real number on your leg. I should have known better. I come from Florida. I know when things bite.

I kept it covered with pants and pretended it didn't exist for a day or two, checking on it each time I went to the bathroom, which is a lot of times, thanks to the IBS I've battled off and on since high school. By day three, I thought maybe it was just a zit, but after poking around with my cheese-tainted fingers, it got bigger, more painful. Something was wrong.

I called Mom and told her about the zit-bite, because she loved this sort of thing. No doubt she was sitting there on my great-grandmother's old twin bed in the Florida room, propping her legs up on a knee-high stack of *Marie Claires* to decode the new braille message that had appeared from the knee down overnight.

"It's not that Morgellons, is it?" she asked me. She used to blame it on bedbugs and the strange things skin does when you have contact with Susie, but lately she blamed any skin problem on Morgellons.

"No, Mom. That's not a real disease."

According to WebMD, it was a totally delusional disease, but Mom had found an online community of depressed middle-aged white women who were also itchy, covered in rashes, and believed they had seen fibers worming out of their skin. Mom had been visiting us last year when she first mentioned Morgellons over pizza at a hole-in-the-wall, telling us it was likely caused by nanobots the government releases in the air or some such babble you'd expect a longtime *Utne Reader* subscriber to tell you over small talk at a pizzeria. *Whatever,* Molly and I said, and rolled our eyes, but she insisted it was real.

"There's lots of websites that say it is," she said now. "I think we have it, you and me both."

"I don't have Morgellons, Mom. Those are conspiracy websites."

"Well, dab some Propa on it then," she said. "Do you have some Propa?"

"No, Mom. Nobody has any Propa."

Her remedy for most ailments until the end of time involves this astringent (Propa pH) in a mouthwash-sized bottle that's been off every shelf except the one in her medicine cabinet since the 1990s. By now, the stuff could strip the pink sponge paint off her bathroom walls. I could sell it to the girls on the street in New Orleans at black-market prices. It could be a choice weapon for their ongoing turf war, which mainly consists of ripping out weaves and leaving them on the asphalt like dozens of dead birds fallen from the night sky.

"Just put some clear nail polish on it," Mom suggested, her next all-time greatest hit.

"I've told you a billion times, Mom."

"Well it works for me, Ms. High and Mighty. Just leave your leg alone then."

I shouldn't have squeezed. I know this. The zit-bite bloomed the way a carnation might when placed in a cup of red food dye, blood slowly spreading to its newly inflamed petals.

The next day I went to Robin's apartment and showed him my leg.

"I think something bit me," I told him.

He didn't care. He was busy with a large painting of a roman bathhouse in his kitchen. He was known for his landscapes, but he was tired of rendering the bruised interstate over Tremé, the pastel sunset thrown over the French Quarter like a cheap Hawaiian shirt. For his upcoming show, he'd decided to move on to things that actually interested him, which, as far as I could tell, involved a lot of procrastination and genitals.

"It looks okay to me," he said, not that he was a great judge of ailments.

In the bedroom, his dog wallowed and whined on the floor, cursed with an awful skin ailment of her own. She constantly gnawed at the skin on her butt until the hair had stopped growing, leaving a blood geyser in its place.

"What do you want to do tonight?" I asked him.

When you date an artist, you don't really go on dates. There are no planned romantic outings for food and cocktails. No trips to the movies, unless he's received free tickets to a film fest because he appears in a terrible scene dressed as a pirate. No concerts, unless you find yourself already downing High Lifes in a bar when the brass band rolls in. Nights usually consist of free red beans, cheap booze, and endless pool tournaments down at the local dive.

"I need to pay my rent before I get evicted," Robin said. "Wanna come?"

"Okay. I'm kind of in the mood for sushi though. Are you in the mood for sushi?"

"I'm not hungry."

Artists never are, until you tell them you can buy dinner. Afterward we rolled up to the slumlord's house. The slumlord was also a flamboyantly gay drug lord and hairstylist with the type of grand-scale plastic surgery that suggests mental derangement. *Gimme the nose on this beauty,* I imagined him telling his surgeon, holding up a photo of a great white shark. His gigantic home was bedecked in gold throw pillows and busts of topless gods. Gold curtains held back by gold tassels revealed a pool out back, placid as a tumbler of blue curaçao. People wanting to buy dime bags or pay rent or get their bangs trimmed mingled around the enormous black marble island in the kitchen, while beautiful young men flitted about, waiting to model their junk for the slumlord's Penis of the Day LISTSERV.

"Look at yesterday's cock," he said, handing us his phone.

It was a big gay Versailles he had going on over there, where people in pantaloons drank a lot of champagne and occasionally urinated in the halls.

"So you're Robin's girlfriend?" he cooed. "You're a real doll. You know about Robin though, right, sweetie? He's slept with everyone. Everyone." He applied his shiny lip gloss with a small wand and pouted. "Except me."

"You know he's just kidding," Robin said.

"No, I'm not," the slumlord said. "Now give me my money, bitch."

The next morning, I woke to find that the resident woodpecker drilling the telephone pole outside my window at dawn resembled the horrendous pain hammering away at my thigh. My zit-bite now had a hard white pustule the size of a grain of sea salt.

"Maybe something laid eggs in my leg," I told the cat over

breakfast. She immediately went under the table and puked. As if she'd never had worms, that hypocrite.

I did what any icicle-toothed redneck in my situation would do: I found a safety pin in the bathroom, put it under the open flame of a NASCAR lighter, and jabbed it deep into my leg. My leg throbbed, but the sea salt remained. By lunchtime, it had practically grown its own vital organs and heartbeat.

"What's wrong with you today?" my coworkers went around saying.

"Nothing," I said. After a few hours, I couldn't lie anymore. I called a staff meeting in the kitchen. "There *is* something wrong."

They sighed and rolled their eyes. They'd seen it before: the scabies, the pinkeye, the rash that broke out on my forearms every Saturday after I washed dishes for an hour. My body had been adjusting to New Orleans for the last two years the way somebody else's might to Retin-A.

"Say hello to my little friend," I said, rolling up my shorts. It had these angry little tentacles now like you might find on a killer meatball.

"Oh, it's fine," my boss said. "What is that, a spider bite?"

"That's definitely staph," my coworker Eric said.

"I think you're overreacting," my boss said, which is exactly what he said after Eric cut the tip of his finger off on the meat slicer.

"No, dude, you could die from that," Eric said. "Those lines coming out are the infection trying to reach your bloodstream. My brother had that. It's staph. Go to the doctor."

I went home and made an appointment, and then sat down at my laptop searching for staph infection pictures on the Internet. Never do that.

᠅

The doctor's office was decorated with framed pictures of two toddlers on Christmas day, smiling in front of a giant tree in a giant room with a giant marble staircase. My doctor was nice, but she only wanted to talk about her upcoming ski trip to Aspen.

"You ever been?" she asked.

"No," I said. "But I've seen *Dumb and Dumber*."

She gave me a strange look, then asked me to show her the infection.

"Oh, this little thing?" she said, swabbing the whitehead. She prescribed an antibiotic called Bactrim and told me I had great boots. They were some floppy 1980s atrocities from Thrift City, the slick, sad color of slugs.

"We can't have girls in cute boots walking around town with infections all over their legs," she said. "Now, can we?"

"I guess not."

After a few antibiotics and a good night's sleep, I woke in horror. The redness was gone, sure, but in its place was a white boil the size of a Cert breath mint. It was Saturday, our busy day at work, lines out the door. A call-in now was akin to murdering my coworkers. Still, I pulled on a housedress and flip-flops and went to the urgent care center.

"It has to be lanced," a new and improved doctor informed me.

"My doctor didn't tell me this would happen," I said.

"Well, she probably didn't think it would. The antibiotics do one of two things: make the infection disappear or make it come to a head that needs to be drained, and yours, well . . ."

She brought over a tray of torturing devices and smiled reassuringly. She draped fresh paper over me like a hostess might a table at the Macaroni Grill.

"What's that for?" I asked.

"It's going to be messy, and I don't want to ruin your pretty dress." It was a two-dollar black polyester muumuu from the Bridge House thrift store on Airline Drive, the only thing I had that could actually go with a staph infection.

She smiled and pulled on her gloves, tapped my leg twice. "You can lay back now. You probably don't want to watch."

I breathed. She warned me there was no possible way she could numb the entire area. She was right. As she cut into the abscess and worked out the infectious bile, I stared at a rubber glove dispenser on the wall and blubbered the way only people in muumuus can.

"The frightening thing about staph," the doctor said, "is it's becoming so rampant that it can't really be treated. They can't create antibiotics fast enough, or strong enough, to combat it. It's quite voracious."

The city was, in fact, full of girls in cute boots with infections all over their legs. And while you could take the antibiotics, that didn't mean they'd actually work.

I sat up. Blood and guts were splattered all over the paper and the tools like something a voodoo priestess might put in a keepsake box alongside some baby-doll heads and an owl skeleton for the fall equinox. The doctor packed my leg, curling gauze into the wound, wrapping the whole thing in an Ace bandage. Warm compress, she said. Change the bandages. Have some painkillers. I obeyed.

❦

Not even Vicodin can make months of unread *Harper's* and Lawrence Durrell's Alexandria Quartet relatively entertaining. Robin had given me the first book in the quartet, *Justine*, a few weeks before, telling me it was his favorite.

I called my mother again, forgetting she's the wool sweater of exacerbation. When you have nothing to talk about, she'll answer right away and go on for hours about her Tide rebates and new Margaret Atwood novel. But call in dire need, and you have to scream *Mom, hello?* twenty times into the answering machine before she'd even dream of picking up the phone,.

"I have some sort of staph infection," I said into the machine, ready to hang up.

"Hello?" she answered. "People die from that. You could die."

"I'm not going to die."

"You don't know that."

"I already went to the doctor, and they lanced it, okay? I'm on antibiotics."

"Just take it easy. Where's the infection?"

"On my inner thigh."

"Oh." She got quiet for a moment then. "It's not on your privates, is it?"

"No, Mom. Ew."

"Well, I'm just asking. I mean, what about this guy you're dating. Is he clean?"

"What? Did Molly say something?"

"No. Just that he might not be the cleanest guy in the world."

I'd already dated the cleanest guy in the world back in college, who disinfected his butthole with a witch-hazel-soaked cotton ball every time he took a dump. Robin probably thought witch hazel was the name of somebody he'd slept with in art school. It was only natural I'd want to try dirty on for good measure.

"Mom, please. He's fine."

"Well, I better come up there."

"No. I'll be okay. They gave me painkillers."

"What kind of painkillers?" Robin asked when I called to tell him about my leg.

"Vicodin."

"You should bring me some for the art openings tonight." He didn't seem to think my leg was any big deal. He told me he'd had a lot of friends get staph and it just went away on its own. He believed I could just jump out of bed and walk up and down the ancient cobbles on Julia Street all night long poking in and out of galleries. "You are still coming out tonight, right?"

"No."

He wasn't even showing any of his own work. He just wanted to go schmooze, probably meet up with a Helen or Ann or Mary, one of his many friends erroneously named after Puritans. Instead, I lay in bed watching as my cat, Kirby, chirped at clouds of purple martins taking flight in the dusk, thousands of them fluttering about as the dark gashes of sunset soaked into the sky like a fresh wound dressing.

๛

In the last days of our relationship, I accompanied Robin to his big gallery opening, but it wasn't very fun. My life had come to resemble a line from an awful Alanis Morissette song: *How 'bout getting off of these antibiotics?* I was starting to feel a little disgusted, a little annoyed. I started to notice that the pit stench Robin left on my skin after spooning was not going away even with half a tube of lavender body wash in the shower. I still had a large bill owed to the urgent care center for the lancing. A week before the gallery show, I found Robin in his kitchen down to his boxers, working on a movie-screen-sized Garden of Eden while the dog picked its butt by his feet.

"How are the paintings going?"

"I am really behind. I have a lot of work to do, and I need a model."

"A model?"

"Yeah. I need a vagina for Eve."

"Oh," I said, showing him the bulky ace bandage. "My thigh is still pretty messed up right now."

You know a relationship is over when you're encouraging your partner to stare at somebody, anybody, else's vagina.

"I just need you to sit in that chair," he said, "and spread your legs."

I'm no Sharon Stone. Nobody liked the way my privates looked on Eve anyways. It wasn't nearly as popular as the still life of a cornucopia with gourds. The after-party was a wretched monocolor affair thrown by an architect, where everyone has to wear one color from head to toe. I showed up in fuchsia, Robin in mustard, the type that falls from a burger and forever hardens onto a car seat. Everyone else wore black, except one lone man in a white Elvis suit with blinky lights on the seams. This Elvis was the DJ, and on some sort of drug that prohibited him from playing the full duration of any song. During the intro to "White Lines," the architect cornered my girlfriend Christine and me to discuss his sangria recipe, while Robin escaped out the back door, following an emaciated poet in a black minidress who wanted to chat about German expressionism.

"Come check it out," he came in to tell me a while later. "They've got a Gravitron in the tool shed."

"A Gravitron?" I asked. In my day a Gravitron was a crappy carnival ride that blasted loud dance music, so nasty middle-school girls could dance in front of it with their Yaga shirts hiked up and their self-inflicted belly-button piercings exposed.

"You know," Robin said. "A gravity bong."

"Oh," I said. "Is that what you and that chick were doing out here?"

"Look," he said, high off his gallery opening and whatever a Gravitron does to the brain. "There's going to be a lot of women coming up to me, women who think I'm sexy. Women who want to be with me. That's just how it's always been, okay?"

"Now, that's disturbing."

My friend Christine forced him to ride in the cramped backseat like a child on the way home. He couldn't even figure out how to open the little side window to smoke his cigarette. All he had to do was unlatch it and push it out, but of course, he somehow managed to break a piece of the latch off in his hand. It has never again been located. I keep driving around no more annoyed than usual, as I've become accustomed to the constant clapping, clapping, clapping sound the window now makes as it rattles over the crappy roads of New Orleans.

There is one more thing: A few months after I dumped him, I ran into one of his friends in a café. A cool artist who looked like the chick who shot Andy Warhol. We got to talking and it came up that I was recovering from months of fighting off a staph infection.

"No way," she said. "Did Robin give it to you?"

"Huh?"

"Back when I dated him, he gave me staph. He'd get these little white dots that would just go away, but my butt would be covered with giant sores and this huge bruise for, like, weeks and weeks."

Have you ever had a moment such as this, holding yourself in a café courtyard on the verge of screaming, knowing somebody's butt sores have been transferred to your inner thigh? I got back in my truck and rattled down the street, listening to the sound my broken back window now made, a round of applause from the completely unhinged.

Apples and Oranges

I t was Christmas 2008 and New Port Richey looked dumpier. We drove around Orange Lake, where white guys in do-rags blasted thug rap from their primer-colored cars on Christmas Eve, smoking blunts next to the life-size Christmas cards.

Back at the house, a small path had to be cleared through my bedroom so I could get to the bed. There was another small path cleared to my childhood desk, which had just enough room for my mother to sit with her laptop, surrounded by magazines, stuffed animals, pottery, Pogs, and a coconut monkey coin bank. She'd finally made the room into her office.

"I still would like to get the sewing machine in here," Mom said. "I have enough room to get on my computer, but that freaking asshole's garage is right next door."

That freaking asshole neighbor apparently had powers that allowed him to annoy Mom at all hours of the day, but like a sasquatch, he'd never been witnessed by any other human eye.

I was able to weasel my mother's classical guitar, a never-played wedding gift, from under the bed to practice my Bob Dylan impersonation while dust bunnies collected at my feet like cashmere socks. Molly also brought her fiancée, Chris, and their dogs and stayed at a scary motel by the Cotee River, where junkies left syringes in the parking lot and actually said things like, *Hey, can I ask you a question? No? Well, fuck you then.*

"Molly and Chris won't even stay here," Mom went around saying. "They're spending more time at that motel than here."

Mainly because they could smoke in bed. It was unclear where Chris and Molly would have slept if they had to stay the night here. Mom herself slept in the spare twin bed in the Florida room, having years ago adjusted to the single life of common-law marriage. I guess she could have shacked up with John for a few nights to oblige, but no, she resorted to the college-roommate solution: *Well, geez, it's not like we have a shortage of couches.* They'd even kept Sheldon the Cat's personal couch, though he'd recently passed away, covered with his cat toys. To say John was shattered was an understatement. He presented a Ziploc of Sheldon's catnip cigars and fake mice to me for my own cat to have, as if passing on a family heirloom. Then he showed off the $400 painting he'd commissioned in honor of Sheldon, even though he had just lost his job and credit card companies had been calling nonstop.

The day after Christmas, Molly figured everybody could use a little break, so she forced their dogs upon Mom and John, and we headed over to Lakeland. The city was tucked halfway between Tampa and Orlando, as if somebody had located the exact midpoint between the world's crapiness and despair and then announced, *Release the methamphetamines unto these people.* Lakeland was also where Sherry had recently moved.

In high school, Sherry had worked at Checkers with Molly and all the other goths. They'd gone to different universities but reunited for graduate school, sharing an apartment in Tampa decked out in Lady of Shalott posters, corsets, and shelves of sci-fi and cheap fantasy, where we all smoked a lot of weed on stained couches. After grad school, Molly found a job in New Orleans. Sherry stayed in Tampa, got a job as a nurse, hooked up with a boyfriend she'd had in high school, and got pregnant. They got married on a pirate ship, as if to say, *This journey will not only be shaky but rocking side to side as the choppy waters of life bash us from every which way.*

A year into the marriage, Sherry gave birth, but her husband moved back in with his father in New Port Richey, unable to keep his heroin addiction under control. Sherry took a job in Lakeland, where she could live for free in an apartment complex run by her dad and stepmom. Her older brother worked as an inspector at the nearby hot dog factory and lived with his family in the apartments too. Sherry was doing okay, except she was in the sticks, and when you're in the sticks, normal life decisions take a greater toll than they would in other places. Such as dating: She'd met somebody nice, but he was way below her, a man with tattoos on his head who was on the run from the law in Texas and couldn't get a job. So he started watching her son for free. Then he moved in. Then Sherry was pregnant with his baby. Molly had warned us of all this on the drive over.

"That all sounds really fucked-up," I told her. "I don't understand."

Sherry had always been so smart. National Merit like Molly. Good colleges and jobs, and nice, hardworking boyfriends. It seemed like she was on her way to having a decent life, and maybe she still was; maybe she was just hung up by the pitfalls of family.

"Her parents are really into pills," Molly said. "They've always been though."

"Maybe it won't be as bad as it sounds," Chris said optimistically.

We took a turn and rattled down a long dirt road, the dust rising all around us in a choking fashion. The apartment complex was just a bunch of cement-block buildings in a random clearing surrounded by barbed wire, like some repurposed prison. There was a deep gulch that ran alongside the complex, shaded by several big oak trees and longleaf pines. In the shade, tied up to one of the trees, was a panting pit bull. The dog didn't bark when we walked up. He didn't get up. He just lay there, looking at us in a way that seemed to say, *I am going to die here, and I'm learning to accept that.*

"That's the dog we rescued off the highway," Sherry said, greeting us in the crabgrass and sandspurs. Her hair. It had always been beautiful, the preordained hair of the goth—long, dark, and wildly curly—and it probably still was, though she had it tied up in one of those hairdos of the damned, not really a ponytail, because the person got too exhausted to pull the hair all the way through. "We think something's wrong with him, so we're keeping him outside."

She gave us a tour of her apartment. A few fairy posters had stuck around from college. There were plastic baby toys everywhere, and she had the type of couch you don't sit on without checking to see if it's dry first. Lots of things squirmed around on the floor: her baby, her slutty cat, and a battery-operated ferret ball that interested neither. Molly and Sherry exchanged candles, the present every girl gets a friend they no longer really know. We sat around in the glow of a very fake Christmas tree, the TV tuned to the USA channel, an airing of the holiday classic *American Wedding*, the grotesque third in the *American Pie* threesome.

"It's great to see you guys," Sherry said.

It was good to see her too. She was healthy at least. I couldn't imagine how somebody who'd plotted her escape from the clutches of New Port Richey over endless clove cigarettes in the Denny's parking lot and had gone on to get a master's degree and a decent job could end up someplace like this. But I thought of my mom then, back in the House of Hoarder, and I felt really depressed. It could happen to anyone. It could happen to us. I'd been in the same class as Sherry's younger brother, a nice kid who always wore socks with sandals, and he'd escaped. Gone to a bigger city, dropped out of college, and forever worked a managerial position in the service industry, but still, it was a measure of freedom.

That's when Sherry reached under the table and pulled out a large purple bong. She looked at us very cordially, very pregnantly, and said, "You guys want to smoke? They say it's okay to have a little when you're pregnant." She rested the bong against her belly and took a long deep hit, coughing. "There's no scientific proof that it does anything, you know, bad."

Her two-year-old son smiled at us from his bedroom door, showing off a plastic gun he'd gotten from Santa, which he then put in his mouth, pulling the trigger.

"I'm gonna go have a cigarette," Chris said, excusing himself outside.

My list of life's most shameful moments had been growing exponentially lately, but I didn't want to knock "attending Limp Bizkit arena tour in a halter top, 1999" out of the top five, so I went with him. In the communal crabgrass, two kids were arguing over a rotten orange on the ground, and I took the harsh first drag of a Lucky Strike.

"That's nasty," one kid screamed. "Don't touch it. It's gonna make you sick."

"What is it?" the other kid asked.

"It's an apple," he told the younger boy.

I'd tutored inner-city schoolchildren since I moved to New Orleans and worked numerous summer camps before that, but never had I seen a kid who couldn't tell the difference between apples and oranges. This kid was at least six years old and didn't know what an orange was. Neither did the other kid, a bit older, probably around eight.

"It's nasty. Don't touch it," the older one said again. Then he picked the orange up and chucked it against the side of the building. They both howled with delight. *Nasty*, they screamed, *nasty*. They wandered by the gulch, squatting near the dog.

"Don't be doing that," somebody yelled from the doorway.

There stood the man with tattoos on his head, holding a beer in one hand and Sherry's son in the other.

"Yeah, don't be doing that," another guy behind him said.

The kids wandered off, following the edge of the gulch to where nobody could see them anymore, as the man with tattoos on his head gave me the international nod of *wassup*.

"Hey. You Molly's sister?"

"Yeah."

"I think you probably know who I am. But this here is Wayne."

"Wassup," Wayne said. He had on a University of Florida shirt. He looked about the age of a college student, but he wasn't one, and probably never would be.

"How's it going?" I said.

We sat on lawn chairs and sunned ourselves for a few minutes, watching Sherry's son aim at and shoot invisible enemies. An old man in a wifebeater and brown polyester pants walked up and poked around a Dumpster at the edge of the woods with a metal detector, swinging it over weeds, trash, and shards of broken bottles. The man with tattoos on his head acted like this was the most normal thing he'd ever seen, but one look at Chris's striped pink socks and cycle shoes and his lip curled.

"What's with this guy?" he asked me.

"This is Chris. Molly's fiancée."

"I can get one of those Lucky Strikes from you." It was more of an order than a question, and he stared at Chris's socks some more before letting it go, whatever was floating around behind the tribal markings on his forehead. "Y'all live in New Orleans, huh?"

"Yeah," we said.

"You ever go down to, what is it, Bourbon Street?"

"Not really," I said. "It's kinda touristy."

"I heard it's wild as shit. I'm trying to convince Sherry to go."

"But I'm pregnant," Sherry said from the doorway. She came and stood over him, massaging his neck, pinching it really.

"So?" he said.

"Yeah, if you're pregnant it's not really a great place to be," Molly said.

"Well I heard Bourbon Street is pretty fucking fun," the man with tattoos on his head said after a while, staring toward the gulch. I could picture him there in the French Quarter, buying one of those stupid shirts that says *I got bourbon faced on Shit Street*, eating cold pizza under the harsh fluorescent lights of an all-night daiquiri shop while Sherry sat patiently beside him, her ankles swollen to the size of Easter hams.

Just then, the dog let out the saddest sound I'd ever heard and went quiet again.

"That dog just wandered up here while the kids were playing," the man with tattoos on his head said. "If it ain't one thing, it's another, know what I mean?"

I did indeed. I understood plain as I had the moment we rolled up here. The same as I did as we rolled on out back to the House of Hoarder, where Mom was on her laptop tinkering around on Ancestry.com, ignoring the wadded wrapping paper all over the house, which sat like a field of giant burrs, waiting to be ironed flat and used again next year.

"Not that you all care," she said. "Leaving me with the dogs while you go off and do whatever you like."

Even back in New Orleans, I wondered how I'd pay my rent, my bills backed up for months. I didn't make any money. I had nothing, but I was free, freer than most. I had a Telecaster anyways, and I let her rip.

Months later, Sherry called Molly to tell her that Dustin, her husband in New Port Richey, had overdosed. He'd died in the very same house, on the very same living room carpet, in the very same manner his mother had a decade before, strung out on black-tar heroin. He never even knew Sherry was pregnant again by another man.

"I saved the obituary," Mom called to tell me. "I cut it out for Molly, so I'll bring it next time I visit."

Instead, she put the obituary somewhere and couldn't ever find what she'd done with it. Molly didn't care. She seemed apathetic about the entire thing, shrugging it off. I myself never even knew who Dustin was. If I remembered back to the goth years—Molly's and Sherry's prom dates, their nights spent going to dance at the Castle, or just seeing them in the lunch commons with their combat boots and dirty looks I couldn't remember him. I leafed through Molly's senior yearbook to look him up, but he wasn't pictured. There was a photo in the back of the yearbook of Dustin and Sherry together though, holding hands in the distance as some popular kids posed for the camera during homecoming 1995. On closer inspection, it might not have even been them at all, but two other random kids dressed in black, stuck forever in the background, their faces just a blur.

Gut-Bomb City

H ave you ever waited in line for the bathroom behind six drag queens, two unicorns, a seahorse princess, and an evil monkey on stilts after downing a bowl of spicy-hot gumbo? Have you ever tried to remove a fake fur coat, leotard, and tights in a tiny dirty bar stall even when you're *not* on mushrooms? Have you ever fantasized about installing a flat-screen TV in your bathroom? I have. Because I have IBS—irritable bowel syndrome—and my home, New Orleans, is not kind to me.

The saddest day of my life occurred at the cheese shop where I worked when a subcontractor knocked down the wall to our employee bathroom with a large mallet and pulled my beloved toilet up from the floor like a radish in a Super Mario game.

"We need more room for storage," my boss informed me.

"But, Richard," I said, "I can't use the customers' bath-room."

"Why can't you use the customers' bathroom?"

"Well, I just had Smoothie King, for one thing."

On certain days, I've had to run home to relieve myself where nobody is around to witness such atrocities, except the cat, who turns all 'Nam on the rug beneath my feet, writhing around as if doused in napalm.

When you feel the need to shit uncontrollably, dating is tough. Like your mind, your whole existence is in the toilet, has been for years, and you certainly can't expect to drag someone down there with you. This poor guy, Michael, contacted me after I hadn't spoken to him in two years. He'd just moved back to New Orleans after a brief bout of grad school and veganism and wanted to know if anything cool and cheap was happening on Saturday night. We met up at Mimi's, where most of these horror stories begin. It's a popular bar in the Marigny that has great tapas and nightmarish bathrooms. The ladies' room has two toilets that practically face each other and no stalls. There's always the chance some crazy bitch will follow you in and lock the door, drop trou, and sit down on the pee-pee-splattered seat, looking at you like, *What, you pee-shy or something? Sucks for you.*

Michael was a writer. He had the sort of skinny-fat body that seems to accompany moderate depression. The first sprouting of man boob and chin gobbler. He had on a black faded shirt, tight jeans, and cowboy boots, an outfit meant for somewhere else—Austin or New York City. Most guys around here wear unbuttoned shirts, clunky man sandals, and swim trunks in the summer, in hopes of finding a nearby pool and babes too drunk to care about man sandals. Michael went around saying "brutal" a lot, which made him sound like some sort of surfer dude, except he'd just moved from Tuscaloosa and owned more western shirts than a Louvin Brother. At the bar we fought as disgruntled writers often do, with the intention of sending the other home to cry in a bathtub.

"Realism in literature is so played out," he said.

"No," I said. "Annoying stories about talking dogs and magical cans of soup are."

Mysterious activities occur in New Orleans all the time and nobody really cares: High Lifes appear and disappear seconds later, hours pass in minutes, cars are driven home by dogs who piss all over your furniture and want to be let out first thing in the morning. Michael and I had originally met upstairs at Mimi's one Saturday a few years ago, dancing at DJ Soul Sister's Hustle party, but now the party just seemed like a hot, heavy mess threatening to break through the floor. There would be no dancing for us. We sat uncomfortably, debating the imminent demise of American prose, while jabbing at goat cheese croquettes and getting the stink eye from a gutter punk with scary face tattoos at the other end of the bar. Then, as most drunk writers are known to do, Michael started whining.

"I can't find a job," he said. "I'm so poor."

He had some part-time thing at a record store on Bourbon Street, which probably involved a lot of eye-rolling and trying to get drunken bikers to stop touching the Lucinda Williams poster.

"Look at me," I said. "I handle cheese all day. Do you think I want to smell like this?"

"I'd rather smell than have no money."

"You think I have money? Ha. Hahahahahaha."

Since he was a year younger than me, I told him what to expect when he turned twenty-eight. The last bit of dreamy youth would finally escape him. His skin would get zittier than a middle-school dance, and his legs would pain him and emerge overnight with hideous blue veins like jellyfish trapped beneath the surface of his skin. He'd have to break down and purchase service clogs to keep his back from giving out. He thought that was ridiculous, *brutal* even. I concurred, realizing that these things only happen to women in their twenties, so I apologized and left to cry in my bathtub.

He'd probably be fine. He was a dude, and dudes are always fine, even if they only own a hairless dog and saggy old beanbag chair like my last boyfriend, who survived off American Spirits and the free wine handed out at gallery openings. And since Michael didn't know my dating history—or that in the past few months alone I'd accidentally crapped my pants four times—he called again, wanting to hang out.

Most of my pants-soiling seems to happen at twilight, when the mosquitoes cloak your dewy skin like chain mail and the sun goes downhill fast, slitting the sky's throat on its merry way. That's when I usually go running up the streetcar line to Audubon Park.

I've lost two pairs of shorts, four pairs of undies, and one pair of New Balances in the past few long runs alone. Some call it the runner's trots, this overwhelming feeling of cannonball blasting through poop deck. I call it painful, the initial intestinal cramping. It's embarrassing, since you never know when you're going to lose it. One time my iPod was blasting Salt N Pepa's "Push It" when the bottom dropped out, so it's possible my body was simply following direction. Sometimes I lose it within feet of my front door, my body so excited about the proximity of a toilet that it can no longer contain itself. Other times, I'm miles away from home, and I must stop and cross my legs behind a small spiky shrub. There's always a small spiky shrub. You can hope people don't notice you, but imagine a soda can being shook up for an hour before you open it. People always notice. Then there's the Charlie Chaplin–style walk of shame back home afterward, the britches fully contaminated and weeping.

Even when I was growing up in Florida, I always had a blowout before cross-country and track events. There's not a mom in the god-awful state who hasn't knocked on the stall or port-o-let door, asking, "Honey, you okay in there?" It got so bad I had to see a doctor when my mother suspected I might have an ulcer at seventeen years of age. I didn't. I just had severe gas. It never stopped. When I lived in North Carolina during graduate school, my then boyfriend would laugh hysterically when I returned home twenty minutes into a run to fumigate the slugs from inside the walls.

"Geez, babe," he'd say. "Maybe you should go see a doctor."

I suggested the same for his Star Wars Galaxies online role-playing addiction. Instead, he started up a long-distance relationship with some droid in Mos Eisley, and I ran for New Orleans, where my sister lived and where I knew I could embrace my inner freak show in the land of gut bombs: coffee and chicory, deep-fried everything, Sazeracs, boudin, crab boils, shrimp remoulade. I can't refuse any of it. Popeyes chicken, Zara's po' boys, raw oysters at Cooter Brown's, and duck-fat fries at the Delachaise. A year in, somebody played a cruel joke on me and gave me a monthly restaurant review column for a local magazine, so I now even get paid to be bloated and in pain.

To get rid of most enablers on my list of shit-triggers would be to deny myself any enjoyment in the indulgent world of *who dat*s and *where yat*s. In other cities across the world I'm sure people find lots of fun things to do besides eating and drinking, but in New Orleans, that's not an option. Show up at a bar for one drink and you're suddenly wrangled into a night of free crawfish or red beans. Show up to race a 10K and they feed you free beer at ten in the morning.

Anyways, food isn't the only issue. Other things set me off too: nervousness, menstruation, life in general. I've kept a shitter's journal. I've done the dear diarrhea. I've studied my sporadic corporal disorders quite intensely, and all I can say is my body doesn't want me to exercise, date, or ever feel sexy.

This Michael—he was a decent guy. He never stood a chance. He invited me over to hang out at his apartment in the Marigny, showed me the books he was reading, and gave me some stories he wanted me to look at.

"I'm really into fairy tales right now," he said. "Brothers Grimm."

"The disturbing stuff? Dancing in lead shoes?"

"Yes, exactly."

You ever stare at somebody, anticipating mouth-to-mouth, and instead they pat the bed for you to sit down, saying, "So this is my CD collection"? We went to Verti Marte and got fried catfish and mounds of macaroni and cheese in Styrofoam boxes as sweaty as the night itself. We sat close to each other on his leather couch and ate food nobody has ever before eaten sober, staring at his roommate's bizarre giraffe statue and listening to nasty cats get their sex on in the street.

He said, "It's so great to have an actual, like, real friend here. You know? You're my first good friend in New Orleans."

"Yeah?"

"Yeah."

We tapped beers. It would have been the perfect time to tap something else, but detecting something unsavory, Michael bolted from the couch. "Would you like to hear some songs I recorded back in Alabama?" he asked. "Some folk songs?"

"Folk songs?"

"Folk songs. The girl I sang with is really good." They were folk songs based on fairy tales. Even the cats outside the door let out a long-winded *ew*.

"So," he said, fetching a new beer and cracking it open. "My ex-girlfriend and I are playing on the same kickball team, and it's really weird."

Usually before the bottom drops out, you start to sweat, fever overtakes you—these wretched, sweaty hot flashes and that all-too-familiar rumble, little waves lapping at the shore before the big ones come and erode the soil.

"I'm so sorry to do this," I said, showing myself to the door, "but I better get going."

"Oh. It's not because I brought up my ex, is it?"

In every single man there is, and will always be, an ex-girlfriend kickball team, and you will never, ever defeat them, turdy butt, so don't even try to play that game.

"No," I said, and hurried down the street to my truck. "Not at all."

❧

I've researched IBS extensively on the Internet. IBS has a Facebook page, but it's not really something you'd want to be friends with. WebMD suggests that IBS may have to do with that weird white sauce on your nachos, sure, but also with emotional stress. Like living paycheck to paycheck, having unmanageable bills and student loan debt bigger than a small island, accumulating endless rejection, and the inability to find meaningful relationships—basically, your late twenties and early thirties.

Symptoms include bloating, abdominal pain, lots of diarrhea, and—big surprise here—depression. Most treatment advice is to exercise and cut back on stress—as if stress is just some little piece of fat on a pork chop you can easily pare down with a knife. As if exercise never caused anybody to superfluously soil herself in public. No more dating broke artists who wear velveteen pajama bottoms in public or talking on the phone with Mother about her scalp picking. Best to stop waking up, even—because they recommend cutting back on coffee too. As if you could rise from your lonely, cat-hair-covered bed while the construction workers rebuild the house across the street and the downstairs Chihuahua shrieks like a crazed Selena fan-club member, and face another ten-hour day of asking people if they want chips or salad with their Gruyère sandwich without twelve cups of dark roast and a nice scream in the bathroom mirror first.

Michael had never seen my search history.

He still wanted to hang out. He rode his bike thirty minutes across town wearing jeans in July to see my band, the Green Demons—a psychedelic surf-punk group consisting of me and four middle-aged dudes—play our first show at a French bistro at four in the afternoon. He stood in the back while we played. He sweated uncomfortably, watching as my friend put on roller skates and cracked her head open on the tile floor.

"All the people in there looked like a bunch of seventies porn stars," he said afterward, probably because all the middle-aged dudes had on little shorts and tank tops, their hair, if any, in stringy ponytails.

"Those are my friends," I said.

"I'm sorry," he said. For what, I was unsure.

Still, he wanted to join my writing group. He wanted to read my stories. He wanted to drink beer, talk politics, have inside jokes. He called me every day and texted silly little nothings, and bestowed upon me the kind of attention that generally accompanies the demise of platonic friendship. Where was this all leading? What were his intentions? Why was he calling me after he'd already made plans to come to my house on a Saturday night to drink some beers, saying nonsense like "My roommate is going to come along too"? When men cock-block themselves, has that ever been a good sign?

﹠

It was a full moon, steamier than a Vietnamese omelet. Michael was already a little tipsy upon arrival, but this still could not explain why he brought the roommate. To make matters worse, the cock block was distractingly hot, not the type of looks you'd expect from a poet.

"I'm from LA," the roommate explained on the way up the stairs. You could see how he'd been tainted from being forced to live in Alabama for a few years during school. He was wearing a gingham shirt and cowboy boots and had a slightly chipped tooth, but nothing about his outfit suggested he'd rather be anywhere else than right there, in my apartment, forever and ever. Michael stopped at an acceptance letter on my wall, my first publication, which the Star Wars boyfriend had framed for me one Christmas.

"Oh my god," he guffawed. "Framed? Ew. Really?"

"It was a gift. My first publication."

We had a beer on my balcony. Since they both had on cowboy boots, I put mine on too. We decided to go to St. Joe's for another drink. As we went downstairs, I realized they'd left my door wide open.

"Did you guys not shut the door?" I asked Michael.

"Um, I don't know," he said.

"Yeah, I don't know," the poet said.

"What if my cat got out? Oh god. My cat," I said. I ran back upstairs and called for her, but of course she was gone. I suppose this is every dude's worst nightmare. Michael squatted in the alley and stuck his head under the house, calling for Kirby.

"Just go," I told him. "I'll call you. She's not going to come out while you're here. She hates people."

"She does?"

"Yeah. Men especially."

After they left, Kirby emerged from under the house, very content, her fur sparkling with dirt crystals in the moonlight. I got her inside and called Michael. I was that lonely. He came back to the house to pick me up and honked. He had one of those old hatchbacks that look like you can't wash them anymore without the paint coming off.

"Where's your roommate?" I asked, getting in.

"At the bar with his girlfriend."

"Oh," I said.

He touched my leg then, the part that wasn't knee-deep in empty Red Bull cans and Nestea bottles. "I'm sorry about letting the cat out. I thought there was going to be another door at the top of your stairs."

"It's fine," I said. I couldn't really blame him. For dudes, there usually is another door waiting at the top.

"Well, what should we do now?"

"We could go see Quintron."

"I can't afford to," he said. "I'm completely broke."

"Mod dance party?" I suggested. "It's free."

"I don't like the mod dance party," he said, but we wound up there anyways.

There were maybe a dozen or so people bopping around

the icky floor in Saturn Bar. Practically empty, since it's not the type of place anybody goes to before midnight. Some crazy girl with her boobs hanging out of her tank top ran up to Michael and started hugging on him, screaming about how much Alabama sucked and how good it was to see him. He didn't introduce me.

I found a seat at the bar and bummed cigarettes from some kids who worked at a sushi restaurant near my house. They were both in their black work clothes. High Lifes appeared and disappeared.

"This place is haunted," one of them said. "You know that?"

"No," I said.

"No, really. My friend was, like, waiting for the bathroom once behind a guy, and after fifteen minutes he finally busted open the door and the guy was gone. It was a ghost, man."

"Man," the other one said. "That ghost sounds like a dick." He turned to me. "Hey, are you okay?"

It was happening. The monstrous beast was awakening from the bottom of the abyss. What had I eaten for dinner? Salmon, steamed broccoli. A sleeve of Ritz crackers and half a tub of Rouses' Cajun krab dip. A hazelnut Ritter Sport. Why, why, why?

"I need to talk to you," Michael said, grabbing my arm as I rushed to the bathroom.

"Not right now," I said.

Except somebody was in there taking her sweet time doing lord knows what. I waited. I waited and waited. Then two girls came up behind me.

"You in line?" a tall, skinny brunette asked me.

"Yeah," I said. I felt really bad for this girl. Not only did she have on a tube top, the sausage casing of skanky fashions, but in a few minutes she would walk into the malodorous ramifications of my IBS—if a bathroom ghost didn't kill her first.

Her friend, a portly Asian girl in a baby-doll dress, smiled at me. Beyond her, the crazy boob girl danced her mess around, doing the camel walk and whatever else could be done in such tight jeans. Finally, an emaciated mod came out of the bathroom, fluffing her bangs and not holding the door.

I entered, well aware of the task at hand. Best to keep all contact minimal unless I wanted to leave with staph, herpes, or a wet purse, or in need of a tetanus shot. *Your a shit sandwich,* the wall informed me, along with a slew of grammatical errors only nerds like me would fuss over while attempting to defecate in a bar without sitting on the toilet seat. But there were lots of pleasantries on the wall too. *Katie and Kirsten were here.* Like, together, in this bathroom? Dear god. By the time I'd read all the way to *FUCK YOU, TP NAZI,* I'd flushed to the brink of an overflow and washed my hands with water hot enough to scald a baby, holding the door for that poor girl on the way out.

Back at the bar, Michael was crumpled over a full High Life. I touched his back and he sort of jerked away. We sat uncomfortably for a few minutes.

"You've been acting really weird all night," I said. "What is wrong with you?"

"Look. I have to tell you something. My ex-girlfriend is here."

"That crazy booby girl on the dance floor?" I asked. She was now working her way behind the turntables, simultaneously dancing, massaging a DJ, smoking, texting, and holding a drink in the crook of her elbow. She was Party Robot.

"God, no. That's just this girl from Tuscaloosa."

"Oh."

"I just feel bad because she's probably been watching us."

"Well, which one is she?"

"I don't see her. Maybe she left."

It was starting to get packed and heatstroke humid, with dozens of people filing in through the dingy protective plastic in the doorway. After a few minutes of staring at my beer, I saw her emerge from the crowd. She came up and tapped him on the shoulder.

"Hey," she said.

It was her. The girl who walked into my shit scent.

The thing about Saturn Bar is it can be dead empty, and you can check your phone, pick at your nails, then close your eyes and sigh, and the second you open them again it's pulsing body to body and there's a loose dog licking your boots. A few hours ago, they'd been white leather and covered in sticky energy-drink residue. Now they were gray suede. Michael was deep in conversation with the ex, so I went and stood outside under the neon sign, called a cab, watched some gutter punks pick apart a tamale, and disappeared into the night.

Sorry I bailed, I texted him. *Have fun.* And maybe he did. Maybe he held his girl in his arms. Maybe they talked about kickball, or jumped onto the dance floor to do the low squat during "Twist and Shout," or parted ways after a few minutes and never spoke again.

I'd like to think they went up to the balcony, sat close, held hands, let their legs dangle over the crowd of sweaty mods. Maybe she leaned in and snorted, "That girl you were with."

"Yeah?"

"She did a number in the bathroom. Like really, really bad."

"Brutal."

And maybe it was brutal, because I found myself back home on yet another Saturday night, completely alone, devouring the rest of the Cajun krab dip and actually thinking Michael might text me back. I played some Allen Toussaint on the greasy kitchen boom box and made myself a massive grilled cheese. By then the booze was wearing off. Reality was setting in. A look in the bathroom mirror revealed I did in fact look like a woman who'd just shat in a bar and left alone.

"Tonight was a horror show," I told Kirby, drawing myself a bath as she shredded the rug below. I soaked beneath a thick layer of Mr. Bubble foam like the twelve-year-old I am and will always be. I went to bed, listening to the wind in the drapes, the Chihuahuas, cats, and roaches skittering about in the night, but never the phone vibrating with a text message.

III.

Adult-Sized Caboodles

The Mother Load

Mom and John drive twelve hours from New Port Richey to New Orleans in their Ford Focus, a hand-me-down from John's elderly mother who can no longer drive. The little car has decent gas mileage, a dozen throw pillows, and air-conditioning that craps out around Tallahassee, so they arrive with steam pouring off their backs fajita style. They fog up the French doors, greeting me with the foreboding welcome proffered by most houseguests sent from another dimension: *We're here.*

It's nobody's vacation or birthday. It's the dead of summer, July. People don't visit New Orleans in July unless they have to. I know that firsthand. But given the recession and lack of jobs back in Florida, the only option John, unemployed for the last seven months, has to find architecture work is to interview at firms nine hundred miles from home.

Usually they stay at my sister's house in the Ninth Ward,

but Molly's pregnant, a good excuse for Chris to gut the guest room for a nursery the moment the in-laws cross the Orleans Parish line. Mom and John couldn't afford to fly. My mother herself doesn't like to fly, or travel really. We never took family vacations, just nice long guilt trips. Now they can't spring for a hotel either. There wouldn't be enough room for them anyways. My mother brings fourteen pieces of luggage for a four-day trip.

My stairs aren't what you'd call *up to code*. There's really no such thing in New Orleans. They wind sharply and steeply, as if searching for the other half of their DNA strand. Then the cat likes to imitate a frozen turkey near the bottom, in hopes you'll trip over her and smash your head through a French door, so she can jump out and escape.

After a quick restroom break, up the stairs and over the cat comes poor John with totes of canned soup and cake mix, and lunch boxes of yogurts and tangerines. There are paper bags full of mixed nuts and fruit snacks, enough Clif Bars to sculpt a Dr. Huxtable, and coolers of Cokes and water bottles. Mom and John never step foot outside without a fresh water bottle and a full pack of Chiclets. Life, for them, has always been about hydration and fresh breath, even if they haven't gone to a dentist in thirty years.

"You know your mother." John shrugs and is off to haul up his suitcases, pillows, blankets, and shaving bag. These days, he's a big guy with a plethora of Life Is Good shirts, a full head of silver hair, and bright blue eyes. Though right now, he's bright red and breathing like a marathon runner, handing me a lumpy plastic bag full of key limes.

"When you go down next get the TP," Mom commands him.

Mom is the authority on Life Is Good apparel. She tells him which shirts to buy and when to wear them.

"Can I just rest a second, Margie?" he asks.

"Goddamn it, John, go."

"Goddamn it, Margie, let me rest a second!"

"You haven't eaten since Panera Bread," Mom says. "You're starting to get cranky."

They always stop at the Panera Bread outside of Mobile. It's their special place. But that means John hasn't ingested anything besides a few snack-sized Snickers in the past two hours.

"Are you believing that?" she whispers to me as he retreats to the living room with his iPhone, his water bottle, and a handful of Chee Wees. "He's such a baby."

Then she picks at the back of her scalp. One day she'll eventually reach her brain. Until then, she looks like she's imitating a gorilla in deep thought.

"That looks painful," I tell her.

"It is painful," she says. Her scalp burns, bleeds, cracks, and crumbles. Her shoulder has a repetitive stress injury from holding her arm up to pick, which is why she now alternates hands. Ambidextrously picking. A bald spot resides at the crown of her head that she camouflages by pinning her thin hair back.

"Mom," I plead. "Stop with the scalp. For the love of god."

"Yes, master," she says. She takes a swig of soda and returns her hand to her scalp. She doesn't even know she's picking. It's just part of who she is now. "I brought this Estée

Lauder makeup case for you to have, honey," she says. This is her favorite thing. Her doling out of possessions. Her agenda of giving.

"Oh," I say.

"You don't want it?" she asks. "I guess I can give it to Molly."

"Hey." Suddenly I got soul and I'm super bad. "Gimme," I squeal. "Gimme."

It's these little sycophantic acts of hoarding I've never been able to deny my mother. I take the makeup case in my arms like it's a new member of the family. There's no makeup inside. It's just a big, empty Caboodle for grown-ups, so big I can keep my Caboodle from childhood inside, but I don't. I put my childhood Caboodle on top of my adult Caboodle in the corner of my bathroom, so now there's a Caboodle stack with a basket of towels on top. In other words, I'm never getting laid again. I can't invite dudes back to my apartment with this sort of desperate premarital towel arrangement showing up all malignant, destined to spread. They'll run away before they've even stubbed their toe on the squirrel toilet paper stand, knocked the Farrah Fawcett picture off the wall, and peed all over the toilet seat. God forbid John actually lands a job in the Little Difficult. I'll own more secondhand towels than a French Quarter bathhouse. When my mother pokes her head in the bathroom, she takes a look at my new Caboodle arrangement and gushes, her hand glued to her scalp. "Oh, it's so nice in here, honey bunny," she says, which means they will stay a few days longer to fully absorb its beauty.

Normal people wouldn't be able to clown-car a Ford Focus like Mom, but she simply adds junk to the car like sprinkles to a cupcake. And she always has sprinkles for cupcakes, little candy bunnies and pumpkins that have been on the shelf long enough to cut glass.

She spends the first afternoon baking Funfetti, while John does everything he can to put his back out before his job interviews, hauling up extensive ephemera from the days of puffy paint and Pogs. Dozens of cassette tapes in a Looney Tunes shoe box, which used to house some sweet Tweety Bird Keds. I'm happy to have back karaoke *Grease* and Whitney Houston. Not to mention Debbie Gibson, Jon Secada, Richard Marx, Guns N' Roses, the Beach Boys, Poison, and EMF. Mine was a cassette tape puberty: Snoop Dogg, Descendents, Foo Fighters, *The Beavis and Butt-Head Experience*. It's little wonder the majority of my friends are middle-aged stoners who like to talk about their farts.

In another box, I find some horrible craft projects Mom saved to remind us that cotton balls and Q-tips should be kept away from children except in the case of bloody knees and earwax removal. Popsicle sticks should be discarded after lice checks, not turned into reindeer art, picture frames, or dream catchers. Kids should be taught to let go of their dreams at an early age. Though shaping them into a crummy trinket made to dangle from an El Camino's rearview mirror comes close, all that yarn would be better suited for your cat's intestinal blockage. In a heart-shaped box covered in a print of Victorian bunnies having tea, there are hundreds of tiny bears I collected from the Harvey Edwards craft store for reasons unknown. There is even one tiny bear in a baby-food jar filled with beads, with a piece of paper glued to the lid that says *a bear on beads,* as if you couldn't tell. Is a bear on beads better than a brain on drugs? I know which one Kurt Cobain kept in his heart-shaped box anyways.

But where are the things I really want?

"Where the hell is my Yogi Bear?"

"Oh," Mom says, as if I've just caught her stealing the last gingersnap from a shark cookie jar that plays the *Jaws* theme when you open it. "I brought him to a teddy bear picnic and I forgot him at the lady's house. It was an accident, honey. When I asked her about it, she said she hadn't seen him."

"That thieving hag," I say. "She stole our Yogi Bear."

"I know," Mom says, rubbing my back as if we've just found out I have angina. "Just breathe, honey. It'll be okay."

To make up for the fact that my Ewok is now a widow, she wants me to have a piece of artwork consisting of seventy-two stuffed canvas sacks sewn onto a five-foot-tall, three-foot-wide canvas. There are two things my mother hates talking about—what she really did at Woodstock and why the hell she ever constructed this hideous canvas structure—but they both may have to do with the lingering effects of LSD on the human psyche. This piece of art is a piece of work. It's sort of a cross between a shoe rack and a sad display of saggy white tits—things that belong on *Sex and the City,* not in my apartment. But I take it in. I actually like it. I do. One day my dream of having a room full of Mom's post-hippie weirdo art will be complete. Until then, I'm left to examine her personal eccentricities. Like this: She travels with the giant box her laptop came in.

"Really?" I say. "Don't you have a laptop case?"

"I don't trust them," she says, as if speaking of her siblings or Republicans. "From what I can tell, they don't really work."

From what I can tell, Mom herself has no plans to ever work again. Then there's John, who got laid off this year. So both of them have been locked in the House of Hoarder without solid plans for the future besides watching *Antiques Roadshow* and throwing around the term *early social security*.

Mom isn't always a sugar booger. She is the drill sergeant for America's laziest army of one, John. He can't help that he was stationed in Guam. Before he met Mom in architect school he fell off a building while he was doing construction in St. Pete, breaking a lot of bones and *probably damaging his brain,* if you ask old Sarge. Twenty-two years later and John can't clean his ears, make a sandwich, take his lithium, or drink beers with his one friend, Peter, without first contacting the authorities. *What are you doing in there* is Mom's way of telling John, *I love you, baby.*

When they're not bickering, they're just talking, talking, talking.

I don't know when it happened, when they reverted back to childhood and my sister and I earned our adult-sized Caboodles, but it happened. Mom and John constantly whine, sing, laugh, argue, ask questions they should know the answers to, obsess over kitty cats, nag, nap, sneak candy bars, smack gum, spend their parents' money, forget sunblock, forget these particular shoes give them blisters, have tantrums when they haven't eaten or slept enough, and generally demand far more attention than I can give them. Occasionally, my mother will walk into a room and bust out in a dance. John will bust out his drawing books and show you every building he's ever sketched, following you around and awaiting your approval like an expectant puppy, until, hours into this nonsense, you must yell at him to stop and go lie down. They can't start a conversation without butting into a preexisting one. They can't sit still, yet they refuse to complete the most mundane tasks.

Can I have a beer? will only lead to *Where are the beers, what type of refrigerator is this, I've never heard of this beer, what is an IPA, don't you have Labatt Blue, how do I open this bottle, shit, goddamn it, I hurt my hand trying to open the bottle, can I have a Band-Aid, where are the Band-Aids, there are only these small Band-Aids, you're now out of Band-Aids, do you have paper towels or a rag, I got blood on the rug, I need a rag for the rug, which rag can I use, can I use this rag, I used a beach towel, can you open this beer for me now, do you have a coozie I can use, oh, Kirby took my spot while I was up, is it okay to pick him up, her up, is it a boy or girl?*

Never let them touch the cat.

After a few hours with these two a nap is necessary, but good luck trying. I attempt to escape them by cooking dinner, but Mom wants to know if I need help. She has one free hand to give.

"No," I say. "You just relax."

But she doesn't want to. She's like a roach that won't go away even when the light's turned on. She dances in the kitchen, humming along to the radio, flipping the pages of a magazine. She only has twelve more magazines to go, all of them involving cream-of-mushroom soup recipes and beach houses.

"You don't even know this song," I say. It's a new song by an indie band nobody's ever heard of.

"Yes, I do," she says, and hums even louder and looks like the plastic ballerina from the jewelry box of my youth that is now unpacked on the dining table, one hand atop her head as she pirouettes to the music.

"You can put on a movie," I tell her.

"John!" she screams to the living room. "Put on a movie."

He doesn't know how, so I pop in *Pirates of the Caribbean* for him. After fifteen minutes of looped intro music with Johnny Depp howling over it, he comes into the kitchen with the DVD remote.

"I can't figure out how to make it play," he says. I show him the large red Play button, but he doesn't look. He's too busy showing me how his iPhone can manipulate a simple picture of Mom, so it looks like she's talking, burping, screaming *John, stop it*, her mouth moving around like a broken drawer, just like in real life.

"I can make movies on this," he says. "Pretty neat, huh?"

"John, go away," Mom snipes. "He is so annoying with that phone."

At least half the time, he's preoccupied enough to not exist on our planet. The iPhone has horrible reception. It isn't good for people who just want to talk nonstop, so it wouldn't suit Mom to have one. There's no use trying to read any magazine or listen to NPR. She's full of rebuttal, expert analysis, and live commentary. She talks over dinner, over radio and television, interrupts pivotal moments in film with outbursts like *Those potatoes gave me garlic breath* and *The shark is attracted by their sex juices*—a pretty spot-on plot summary of *Mega Shark vs. Giant Octopus* starring poor old Debbie Gibson.

John's favorite way to watch television is by going to the kitchen and cracking ice during the good parts, so Mom must scream at him to stop because we can't hear her commentary over his soda-makings. In the bathroom, Mom tries to talk to you through the door (*Oh, good, you're using the soap I brought you last time*), or she tells you about the rash she's studying in the mirror (*I think it's from the soap you brought me last time*), or she hums, whistles, buzzes, clucks, chuckles. While brushing her teeth, she gargles and chokes. Always has. You're not getting a good brush in unless you're gagging loud enough for the neighbors to get concerned. Nobody has ever been able to shut her up. Nobody has ever been loud enough to. There is no snooze, no off switch, no mute or muzzle for the mother load. There is no silent night, no holy white noise to drown out her monstrous snoring. Not even the thick wooden foundation of my shotgun can block out that unending turbine. By "shotgun," of course, I mean my apartment.

Who's sleeping in my bed? Mom and John, fresh into their sixties, broke, unemployed, and underneath my blankies. I'm astonished this day has come, that John is interviewing for jobs in New Orleans in hopes of landing one, so they can move here with all their five hundred teacups and four hundred wicker baskets, close to Molly and me, be around us all the time, wanting to do things like go to Jazz Fest, where Mom can yell at girls with dreadlocks to *stay off our goddamn blanket* (it's happened before) and we'll all be one big happy family with heat rash and bathtubs of mosquito water in our back-yards. I put bourbon in my morning coffee, see, to celebrate.

I get a few moments to myself before they steal the paper and hog up the bathroom, even though I have to be downtown in thirty minutes to eat free Eggs Sardou and get ignored by all the other food writers at a James Beard Awards press breakfast.

"I'm worried," Mom says, scuffling into the kitchen in her slippers. It could be a hundred degrees outside and she would still sport those marshmallows on her feet.

"What are you worried about?" I ask. "It's eight in the morning."

"I'm afraid somebody's gonna break into our house while we're gone."

"Why would somebody do that?"

"I don't know," she says, and picks her scalp. "I just have a bad feeling."

Perhaps it's the all-out war she's supposedly waged on the neighbor Bob, to the right, or the stoners down the street with the loose pit bull. She's very sensitive to being attacked. She'd call the cops if a mouse ate her cookie.

"Mom, if the house is in the shape it normally is, they'll probably trip and break their necks trying to get in the door."

"You're right," she says, and finishes off the coffee. "I'll make us another pot."

Never let them touch the French press.

Around lunchtime, we pick John up from his interviews. You shouldn't drive if you're doing stuff on the phone, and John is always doing stuff on the phone. We take him to eat at one of the best restaurants in New Orleans, Coquette, for lunch, where halfway through our meal he realizes he's in a restaurant eating lunch.

"What is this place?" he asks Mom, looking up from his phone. "What is that?"

"Escargot," we say, downing our appetizer.

"We can't afford this," John says.

"Stop talking about money," Mom says. "It's rude." She prefers the elephant in the room to please stay quiet and discreet as it flares its ears and charges our table, only to find our credit cards have all been declined.

"The prix fixe menu isn't that bad," I say. It's no more expensive than Chili's, but I suspect they'd be more comfortable with a hot tub of spinach dip and frozen drinks the color of blended gremlins, followed by a visit to Barnes & Noble, the intellectual hemorrhoid that often troubles a Chili's backside.

"Just have a beer and relax," Mom tells John.

But John doesn't know any of the beers on the list, and it's obvious he can't relax with the anxiety caused by his interviews. He believes he screwed up royally, telling the good-old-boy firm he wanted too high a salary, telling the young hipster firm he wanted too little.

"This little Asian lady asked me if I ever worked overseas,

like, in the Middle East," he says, worried. John's never even been to the mid-Atlantic.

Mom and I split a feta-and-watermelon salad, but John doesn't eat any.

"I'm not very hungry," he says, a sure sign he's freaking out.

"I'm sure it went well," I say, trying to cheer him up. "Most people think their job interview went worse than it really did, right?"

When John knocks his glass of water over and it spills into my lap, I wonder if people aren't usually accurate when they assume things are going badly.

After lunch, we head downtown in the Ford Focus. Most of the throw pillows Mom's stashed in the car are Mary Engelbreit, a brand of quilty knickknackery that must be laced with some pheromone postmenopausal Southern ladies can't resist. *Easy Does It*, a pillow's embroidery cautions before I toss it to the floor. John, who has courteously pulled up the history of New Orleans on *Wikipedia* for iPhone, refuses to stop reading it.

"He's on a roll," Mom says. She keeps picking and picking.

I can now just snap my fingers, and she stops with the scalp for a moment or two. The next step in her treatment will be electric shock therapy, Sinéad O'Connor shave-down, or total lobotomy.

"Your mother refuses to see a doctor," John says. "I keep telling her she needs to see a doctor for that. I told her I'd pay for it."

"Oh, sure," Mom says. "So you can hold that over my head?"

There's really no room for anything else to be held over her head with her hand already taking up the area.

"Hey, Wendy," John asks me. "Have you ever heard of Pinckney's Treaty?"

"Oh, John, shut the hell up," Mom says.

"Everybody should just calm down," I say, and swerve past a pothole big enough to live in. There's a brief moment of silence before John pokes his head into the front and reaches for a grocery bag under Mom's legs.

"What are you doing?" Mom says, swatting at his arm.

"I want those Snickers."

"No, John."

"Gimme a Snickers, Margie."

"We just ate lunch."

"I want those Snickers."

"Jesus, Mom, just give him a Snickers."

"Fine. Have a friggin' Snickers. They're all melted anyways."

Eventually she hands one to me, and she eats one herself. Melted chocolate oozes on my jeans, near the lingering wet spot from John's spilled drink, so it looks like I've thoroughly soiled myself. But Mom is perfectly happy now, humming along to the Lucinda Williams CD. *Are you all right?* Lucinda asks. Well, are you?

"Oh, look, there's a place for rent," Mom says. "Pull over."

I keep going, but ignoring her is not a good tactic. I've been ignoring the fact that they're hell-bent on moving to New Orleans, and look how that's going. I'm not my sister. I can't just put up an invisible wall and separate myself from my mother's shenanigans and bullshit. I feel bad for Mom, but I don't take orders from her anymore either.

Probably the worst place a pack rat can move to is New Orleans, land of bargain centers and backyards turned decaying statuaries. The ubiquitous *Be nice or leave* signs on every door might as well read *Enablers only*. Anyways, Mom can't afford a place big enough to house all her possessions.

"You need to be realistic about your situation," I say. "You should probably look for a job first if you really want to move here."

"I can't," she says.

"Why not?"

"Because I'm going to take care of Molly's baby when she goes back to work."

"What?"

"Yeah. I told her I don't want my grandbaby being raised in some weird day care by a bunch of strangers."

"When did you decide this?"

"We talked about it a few days ago."

"And Molly thinks it's a good idea?"

"Of course she does. Don't you?"

"Um. I guess. Were you just not going to tell me?"

"I just did."

Vampires, velociraptors, and megalodons, armies of rabid ferrets and little zombie kids, giant potholes from outer space, please eat me alive before I have to live in the same city as Mom and John. I si-lently pray John won't get a job here, that they'll stay in Flor-ida. That they will not know the sunset as it turns the sky above Audubon Park the shade of grapefruit, the cold raw oysters at Cooter Brown's on a hot evening, the random trumpeter on foot, the Elvis on a scooter, the sidewalk poet and his typewriter. I consider dropping them off on Bourbon Street, at the Walmart on Tchoup, at Hank's on St. Claude, where you can buy a two-piece fried chicken for a buck and gutter punks stick to the side of the building like fruit flies. Places that will make them want to be back in the land of Sam's Clubs, Hallmarks, and Super Targets. Places that will chase them off.

Don't go to the National World War II Museum if you're already on the verge of crying. It's a great museum, a must-see for history buffs, but it's hard to make it out of there with dry eyes. Tanks, planes, and Higgins boats (at least twenty thousand of them were made here in New Orleans) line the bottom floor. Endearing veterans greet you at the door, so it's nearly impossible for someone like Mom to get in the ticket line after an entire hour of conversation and moseying around the C-47 in the entranceway.

"Stop talking to strangers," I urge her.

I'm pretty sure when I was a kid, she would've given me death threats if I introduced her to strangers and told them all about her. The veteran at the door is just being nice, telling us to try the American Sector, the diner attached to the museum run by celebrity chef John Besh, when Mom's all "My daughter here writes a food column for *St. Charles Avenue* magazine." You should never mention anything about food to a New

Orleanian if you want the conversation to end in the next millennium.

For most scholars, examination takes place in a library or study. For my mother it has always been in a dressing room or produce section, considering every hair on a cashmere sweater or kiwi. This is what it's like to go to a museum with her, searching every historic photograph to see if she can spot a relative. That and she mutates into a historian the second the museum pin is clamped to her bosom. By the time we hit hour two, we haven't made it past the home front and I'm regretting not purchasing an audio tour headset.

"This is part of the reason we became pack rats," Mom jokes, pointing to an exhibit of ration books, coins, and A and B bumper stickers for gasoline provisions. There are posters of women going without panty hose or cuffs for their dresses. "Mommy and Daddy saved everything. We were trained to hold on to every little thing."

"Weren't they supposed to donate stuff to the war effort too?" I ask, pointing to a stack of tires that goes to the ceiling, which represents how much rubber was donated during wartime. She chuckles, and I wonder if for all the times we've ever been to Goodwill, I've ever seen her donate anything.

"Back when I was in Guam," John starts every sentence.

"Stop being annoying," Mom tells him.

Wounded, he disappears for most of the war.

Around the time we hit Normandy and Mom starts lecturing on a great-uncle who was in the 101st Airborne Division, I finally tell her I could do without her commentary.

"Fine," she says. "I won't say another word. How about I also stay twenty feet behind you? Would you like that too?"

"Stop it."

"You're really hard on me. You act like you don't even want me here. I don't deserve to be treated like this."

Here we go. Into the line for a Tom Hanks 4-D movie, *Beyond All Boundaries*. John stares vacantly into the restaurant, Mom pouts, and I chew the last tasteless bit of Chiclet, all of us silently dealing with the holocaust pictures we've just been exposed to. Hundreds of us are stuffed into a small waiting room with one bench offered for the crippled and obese. We are played an introductory movie just like they do before you board a ride at Universal Studios. Large doors magically open with an airy fart, and we're herded into a large, dark theater the temperature of a meat locker for an intense cinematic experience that turns our seats into massage chairs every time a bomb goes off. I'm fairly certain this film would cause horrendous flashbacks in veterans of any war. The man to my left jumps clear out of his chair and knocks his sunglasses to the ground when a kamikaze dive-bombs us. I get motion sickness, practically lose my snails. Finally, fake snow falls from the ceiling and evaporates just above our heads as a soldier in the wilds of winter tundra writes a love letter to his gal back home. I turn then to find my mother in tears. Since the massage chair has knocked loose some old roller-skating injury in the tailbone region, I cry with her. We sit miserable and snot-streaked, our butts forced to jiggle as bombs rumble in the distance. Suddenly our vision blurs as a veil of dry ice creeps in around us. We're deep in a jungle, alone and terrified. Nothing can be seen or heard. There's only the sense of impending doom, and something else. Mom. Digging around in her purse.

"Shh," I say. "What are you doing?"

Her hand appears through the smoke, holding up a wad of crinkled Kleenex.

"All I got are used ones," she says. "You probably don't want it."

"Just give it here," I say.

I take it and dab my nose and eyes. Then I stuff the tissue into my purse, where it shall remain, long after completely falling apart.

You'll Only Be in the Way

hris and Molly abandon their house and head to North Carolina for a spontaneous beach vacation the moment Mom and John move to town. Normally, doctors wouldn't encourage a pregnant woman to travel like this, especially in the August heat, but the stress of having Mom and John around would be even worse for my sister. They don't have a house or apartment lined up. Instead, they've asked to stay at Chris and Molly's house while looking for a rental.

"Take your time and find a good place," Molly tells my mother encouragingly from afar. Then she calls me and hyperventilates into the phone. "Oh god. Oh god. It's a full-frontal assault. I can't do it. Oh god."

"It's your own doing," I remind her.

While John drives the little Ford Focus to his new job in Metairie every day, Mom holes up in Molly's house, lurking on Craigslist and avoiding any listing that requires a credit check.

She's brought a bunch of magazines about homes and gardens with her. She's actually a great house hunter when she can just stay in bed.

I try to help Mom out. I pick her up to look at apartments on a day off from tutoring and the cheese shop. I wouldn't trust her to drive around the city by herself. She's the type of driver who could easily get stuck on the roundabout at Lee Circle, forever going around and around like a dog chasing its tail, afraid to pick a direction, any direction.

After making me wait for thirty minutes in the living room, she finally emerges, doing her usual "How do I look? Does this outfit make me look like a moron or what?"

"No, I think it's the scalp picking that's doing it."

"Lay off."

She says she's very depressed. She's become disenchanted quickly, which is the special secret nobody likes to tell you about moving to New Orleans. Disenchantment is what the Big Easy is made of—she hasn't even had the pleasure of dealing with the DMV or Wi-Fi providers yet—and Mom does seem to have a rather early-onset case.

"Have you even gone outside or anything?" I ask her.

"I went to Walmart," she says. Give my mother a new city, a new state, a new life, and the first thing she'll do is locate the closest Walmart. "They have a good meat department at the one in Chalmette. I found the Big Lots too."

In terms of housing, Mom needs to find the Big Lots of apartments. They can afford only $900 a month, which isn't very promising in the price-gouging capital of the South.

"What is the St. Roch area?" she asks as I start the car. "There are several listings there."

I cross St. Claude Avenue and drive her down cracked streets with buildings wrapped in cat's-claw vines, some of them split open like rotten watermelon or half burned down with only a car seat on the porch.

"This is St. Roch."

"Oh," she says.

We head uptown, toward the land of the unaffordable, passing the big slow ladies jaywalking on Claiborne and the endless road construction. You deserve to take your time in this heat. Everybody deserves that, at least. My mother included. She *is* taking her time, always has been. Even now, we're forty-five minutes late for a viewing appointment in the Riverbend.

The house on Spruce has its own garage. It's big. It's dirty. An artist used to live here with his dogs—you can tell by the scent alone—but he moved to Baton Rouge. It has a yard. It's near St. Charles and Carrollton with their sprawling beautiful homes.

"We could take the streetcar to the park," Mom says.

There is the levee and the bike trail. She could exercise. She could actually leave the house, except there is an abandoned warehouse across the street, where ne'er-do-wells might lurk in the shadows.

"I'm not sure what that's all about," she says, eyeing the overgrown weeds and shot-out windows.

Still, she likes the house on Spruce, and it's only $850 a month. It even has an upstairs bedroom, and a huge pantry in the kitchen for her nuclear-bomb shelter's worth of canned goods. At this price, they'll be hard-pressed to find anything that doesn't have the appearance of a freshly used lint roller.

"I think we should get it. What do you think?"

"Yeah," I say. We send the photos to John, encouraging him to see it in person.

"He doesn't like it," Mom calls to tell me a day later. "He says he wants central heat and air."

He also wants a driveway, a lawn, a replica of the House of Hoarder in New Orleans. My mother wants a cottage by the sea with gladiolus in the front yard and built-in tchotchke shelving like all the photos in the ten thousand white-lady *Martha Stewart Living* magazines she's read. Instead, there is a carpeted apartment where famous chef Paul Prudhomme apparently used to live and a tiny renovated shotgun a block off Bayou St. John, which is smaller than my own apartment. There is a drafty double in the Lower Garden District just out of price range and a life-size ashtray in the Marigny. Something is wrong with every place. Nothing is good enough. Naturally, Mom passes the blame on to John.

"He's making this very difficult. I just can't deal with him anymore. I can't do it."

She's been telling me the same thing for the past twenty years, but she's never left him, never will. For all John's debt and loans and crappy moneymaking decisions, my mom is still very dependent on him, codependent really. He is the only thing keeping her afloat. I try to lift her spirits and take her to lunch at this nice little Cajun restaurant, Boucherie.

In the land of whole-hog specialties, my mother is only interested in sea creatures.

"Are the scallops on the menu bay scallops or sea scallops?" the port authority wants to know, not that it matters. She likes both.

"I get those bags of frozen bay scallops all the time at Publix," she tells me. "I went to Rouses the other day, and I'm not that impressed."

"Yeah, it's no Publix," I tell her. There are no old retirees in hairnets handing out teriyaki chicken samples from a Crock-Pot anyways. Here you get price checks that take longer than the *Titanic* to go down and Igloo coolers of self-serve boiled crawfish so spicy your eyes sting and nose runs by the time you leave the store.

"I'm just so concerned about finding a place," Mom says. "And I don't know what's going to happen with the house in Florida. I'm scared."

She tells me that last year John paid $1,000 to have an appraiser come out to the house so they could be eligible for Obama's refinancing bill, but the appraisal was $3,000 less than they needed to qualify, and she said it just seemed like a big scam. Mom and John literally have nothing saved. What do you tell your parent who, at age sixty-four, currently has $17 in her bank account? "Welcome to the club"?

"It'll be okay," I tell her.

"Sorry. I don't mean to be so depressing," she says, and perks up when the scallops arrive. "Aunt Libby asked me what we're doing moving here. I think she's jealous. She says, 'Now, don't you go down there and mess with those girls' lives,' as if I would do that."

❧

Two days later, she is messing with my life, calling me on the phone telling me she heard my band is playing at the Circle Bar, thanks to the local radio station.

"Should I come?" she asks.

"Sure," I say. "It's going to be really loud though, and probably pretty late. Just warning you."

I forgot nothing is loud enough to drown out my mother. Hours later she's taking over the conversation I'm having with a potential bass-playing manservant at the bar, telling him my failed creative undertakings and drinking more beers than I've ever seen her put down.

"Wendy used to play French horn," she tells him. "And then she was in a folk duo. She was in a musical in high school, *Once Upon a Mattress*, starring role, and almost had to drop out when she sliced the back of her heel open on a screen door."

"I'm sorry, but who is Wendy?" he asks after she's talked to him for a good thirty minutes.

He knows me only as Gwendolyn, and he's too big of a stoner to make the connection that the woman he's talking to is my mom, the person I've been whining about to my friends for the past several months. *She is going to bring all her drama here*, I've been telling them, *and I'm going to have a meltdown.* When my band plays she does the mashed potato in the front row, a real dancing machine.

"Did I embarrass you too much or what?" Mom asks at the

top of her lungs out front after the show. She didn't bring her earplugs or a designated driver, and now she's partially deaf and needing a ride home.

"No. You're fine. Just get in the car."

"What are you all bent out of shape for?" she asks. This is what the drunkest people in the group always ask the ones who didn't keep up.

"I'm just tired. It's three A.M."

"It is? Oh, wow. Hey, the band sounded good, Wendy. Excuse me, Gwendolyn."

"I'm so sorry for using my full name. Why didn't you just name me Wendy?"

"Oh, don't be a stink butt," she says.

After two weeks of searching, they find an apartment on Piety Street in the Bywater, newly renovated and near Molly and Chris's house. It's within walking distance of the drag queen brunch at the Country Club and even closer to Bud Rip's dive bar, which means Mom and John, well into their sixties, now live in one of the trendiest neighborhoods in America.

"And I'm pretty sure our landlords are gay," Mom says.

"What does that mean?"

"Nothing. They're gay, that's all."

Thankfully the gaylords don't have a hoarder radar (not to be confused with the far more common whore-dar). Mom and John surely wouldn't have gotten the house then. Mom drives back to Florida to get the packing under way, while John stays on Molly's couch and goes to work at his new job. He can't stay in the new house because he doesn't have an air mattress or a personal chef.

"He expects me to cook dinner every night," my sister calls Mom to complain.

"No shit," she says. "How do you think I've felt for the past twenty-five years?"

It's a well-known fact that the only thing John knows how to make in the kitchen is a whining sound.

The calls start rolling in from the House of Hoarder the second Mom arrives back in New Port Richey.

"You wouldn't believe what that freaking asshole next door did while we were gone," she says. "He put hundred-pound bags of cement all over the front lawn. There's like a dozen bags out there."

"How do you know it was him?"

"I just do, okay?"

"Well, why would he do that?"

"Because he's a psycho."

My mother has been telling me this for years. Despite living on a rootin'-tootin' strip of broken Jet Skis, lawn-chair grannies, and grown men on children's bikes, my mother never had a real problem with the neighbors until the guy next door showed up. When I was in middle and high school, his house belonged to my friend Andrea's family. We used to hang out on her waterbed, eat shrimp fried rice, watch MTV's *Sandblast*. What he does with three bedrooms and two bathrooms all to himself probably isn't anything more entertaining than that.

He bought the house in 2002 and didn't make much of a stink until three years later, when he knocked Mom and John's garbage cans around like a bunch of mail-order brides one day, running them down in the street with his van. Lord knows everything my mother did to piss him off. She'd never admit to any wrongdoing. If this turf war had its own propaganda campaign, hers would certainly look more like *Southern Living* than *Predator Hunting*, that's for sure. Whereas the things she's accused him of doing over the years make him sound like a distant cousin of the Texas Chain Saw tribe. He's buried wire hangers in the yard, so Mom would slice her legs open when she mowed. He's put large blinking orange-and-white barricades in the fenceless front yard, where he believed the property line was, which of course was not where Mom and John absolutely knew the property line was. The aloe plants and cacti do not fall on his property, despite all their natural prickdom.

"And where do you think he got those barricades?" Mom asked. He picked them off the side of the highway, the way my grandmother used to get wild plums for canning season. *Eat at your own risk, dolly,* Grandma used to warn me, handing over the Bunny Bread and peanut butter. At least she was a resourceful thief. Her jam was delicious. The neighbor's barricades aren't put to very good use, unless you like having strobe lights in your disco yard every night.

He's installed professional-grade surveillance cameras on the side of his house and somehow managed to poison the plants in Mom's backyard. Lemons tanned, wrinkled, and dropped dead faster than most Floridians. The cops even came out, much to everyone's chagrin.

But ask a simple "What did *you* do to *him*?" and you're considered a traitor.

John, ever easy to coax information out of when given a few Labatt Blues, eventually admitted that the neighbor had once tried to hang potted plants on the fence.

"So Margie went out there and took them all down. They got all smashed up."

"Well it's our fence," Mom had hissed. "He can't just hang stuff on our fence."

When bombs are dropped, doesn't war tend to follow?

The neighbor guy has spent years tossing his empty beer cans over their fence, along with lightbulbs, cigarettes, crusty socks, rusty umbrellas, and most things you'd leave rotting in your molester van before abandoning them in a Village Inn parking lot off I-75. It's only natural he'd want to discard his old cement and a single tire with the words *dry rot* spray painted across it on Mom and John's lawn while they were out of town.

"And to top it all off," Mom says, "there's holes dug up all over the yard, and something's been shitting up a storm out there. I don't know if it's a mole or what, so I have to deal with that too."

Could be a raccoon, a snake, or even a *Tremors* worm. Whatever it is, Mom has Grandma's hunting vest and Molly's old green beret from Girl Scouts at her disposal, so she can go full John Wayne on the situation if she wants.

"But I don't have time to deal with any of it," she says. "I don't even know where to start with the packing. This place is a nightmare."

※

Besides the abominable neighbor, there's the problem of what to do with the House of Hoarder itself. John has already refinanced it twice, and that means they can't sell. The house is so far underwater financially it even comes with John's old scuba gear from the seventies. This means they must rent the house to be able to make their mortgage payments on top of whatever rent they'll be paying in New Orleans. Of course all this comes with its own caveat: *We don't want strangers living in our house.* As if strangers could somehow be worse than family members or friends.

The options are limited. Extremely limited. Mom's few friends from the West Pasco Historical Society all have homes. Aunt Libby lives in her Christian retirement community. Susie has a place with an unmarried couple living behind the movie theater where she once punched a lady in the face. That leaves Sherry, with her two kids, and the man with tattoos on his head, who've been staying in a little cement-block duplex off Moog Road for the past few months, having moved back from Lakeland.

"They're looking for a place," Molly calls to tell Mom.

"Well, that could be a good idea," Mom agrees.

Mom takes a break from packing to give Sherry, the man with tattoos on his head, and their kids a home tour. She shows them the big yard, the space Sherry will have to raise her kids. She introduces them to the one good next-door neighbor, Leslie, a sweet lady who works at the Publix Deli and who is finally recovering after being bedridden for months because of an infection she got after a minor surgery.

"This will be great," Sherry assures Mom. "We are so excited."

Sherry's son runs around the backyard and tests out a hammock. They take him inside and show him my old teal bedroom, which will soon be his. He can even have the old surfer posters, the Quiksilver shot of Kelly Slater, the Rob Machado, the epic barrel and the slogan underneath it, which I was raised to disregard: *No Fear.* My mother preferred we stay inside with the doors locked and the blinds drawn, away from the dangers of the outside world. But now, with the curtains packed and the sun shining in, the house on Missouri Avenue seems different. Filled with light, with hope. There is the notion in the air that dreams can come true, that good things do occasionally happen.

"But just beware," Mom says, never one to let a foreboding moment go to waste. "Some of the neighbors are, you know, not the best people in the world. It's mostly rentals, so you get what you get. I'm just glad to have someone responsible like you moving in."

She shows them the yellow prefabricated house across the street that's been vacant for a year, the grass waist-high. At least four people live in another house across the street from Mom, where Andrea's aunt used to live. Andrea's aunt Susan was a fluffy-haired softball beast of the six-foot-four variety. Her husband, a shrimper, had three actual nipples. Going inside their house to babysit was like opening the wrapper of a cheeseburger that's been stuck under a car seat for two months. It couldn't be much worse than that.

She shows them the rednecks across the street, who don't cause trouble, though their gigantic pickup truck with hot-tub-sized wheels and their John Deere are extremely loud. She shows her the house at the end of the block inhabited by a handful of Mexican men, and across from them, an even smaller house, where sometimes a little old man comes out back without a shirt on to hang things up on a clothesline. She shows her where the druggies live, yards of red Trans-Ams and dead plants. She shows her the neighbor's surveillance camera.

"He's a real asshole," she notes.

The next week Mom finds a hypodermic needle in the front yard while checking the mail, and then a pit bull squeezes under the back gate and tears through the backyard with a German shepherd nipping at its legs. Mom's yard has always been full of lavish plant growth, the part that hasn't been poisoned anyways, something that comes natural to most Florida natives. A knack for growing plant upon plant upon plant has always been a means to block out the encroaching modern world. Even Aunt Susie, whom you'd expect to grow hypodermic needles in her front yard, has a green thumb and has had a beautiful yard everywhere she's ever lived. The dogs scalp the grass from the earth, trash the basil plants, the tomatoes, the peppers. Pots crash, sending shrapnel all over the patio. A birdbath lifts from the ground like a mushroom cloud and falls hard, drowning the gory aftermath of the rosebush in slimy mosquito larvae and stony shards.

Mom swings open the back door in her towel turban and snarls. There are people in the world who can intimidate dogs, and there are people who can intimidate dogs even when clad in a frilly nightgown and slippers. My mother is of the latter breed. Coupons in one hand, broom in the other. I've never even seen her use the broom for anything except scaring animals. And I've never heard her refer to a pit bull without using a *freaking* first.

"Who let the dogs out?" I sing when she calls.

"Those bastards down the street."

"Which bastards?"

"I don't know. I don't know any of these people. I think they belong to these kids living in the house on the end of the block. You know Misty's sister's house?"

It's a small, sorbet-colored home that could've been really nice if it didn't have a sand yard. Mom's neighbors only like to keep grass in their nightstands.

"I'm pretty sure they're selling drugs," she says. "One of them is black."

"Just because a guy is black doesn't mean he's selling drugs."

"Well, this guy's got dreadlocks."

"Well at least he has a job. That's better than like ninety percent of Pasco County."

"I guess you're right about that."

Since Mom is home alone, without even a Michael Jackson

cutout (alas, we only had an Ace Ventura one that rotted years ago) or a blowtorch or one of Grandma's old rifles, she opts out of a counterattack.

She busies herself with packing, inviting over Aunt Libby to help her, which means sitting around eating potato salad and talking about the good old days, looking through photo albums one at a time before they're slowly layered into their bubble-wrap nest. It takes her months to pack everything. John and Chris fly from New Orleans and rent a U-Haul to bring their belongings back to the new apartment. Molly is way pregnant, so she sits out from the moving fun, and I'm banned. Not allowed to come help because Mom says, *I don't want to hear it*, and *You'll only be in the way.*

The man with tattoos on his head comes over to help them load the U-Haul on Thanksgiving Day in exchange for beer. I'm happy to stay home and eat endless turkey with my sister in peace.

"Well, I'm not cooking," Molly tells me. "For anybody."

It takes two whole days to load the U-Haul and John's truck with belongings, and even then my mother has things stuffed in the garage and in two storage spaces. The man with tattoos on his head takes a break and cracks open another Bud, surveying his new garage, all the things Mom and John will leave behind: furniture, gardening shears, the mower, and tools. Things most people would never leave unattended in a home they're renting out.

"Y'all just gonna leave this?" he asks. "Not packing it up or nothing?"

"We'll have to come back for it," John says. "Sorry about

that. We just don't have room right now, or time to deal with it."

"No worries," the man with tattoos on his head says. "I could use some of this stuff to keep the house up."

"Well, yeah," John says. "Just be careful with it. A lot of this is pretty valuable, you know?"

The man with the tattoos on his head smiles and tips his beer toward John. "Sure enough, hombre, don't have to tell me that twice."

The Other South Beach

I sure enjoyed my trip to Cocoa Beach. It was so
great to see everyone. I hope we can do it again
soon. I love your new boyfriend. He seems like a
keeper. I hope we didn't chase him off. Everytime I
had a new boyfriend I worried about the teasing,
but Bob, my first husband, I should have kept him.
He is still so good-looking.
—Aunt Libby, August 2011

For the last decade, my sister and I have been going to the South Beach Inn for summer vacation. Despite its name, the motel is not in Miami but in Cocoa Beach, Florida, an area of Brevard County mostly known as the birthplace of pro-surfer Kelly Slater and prop-comedian Carrot Top. It's a place that comes with both the good and the bad. There are giant gaudy surf shops, an adult superstore the size of a mall, and a warehouse where you can buy seashell toilet seats among many sad tropical birds. There are always people on the beach wearing boa constrictors around their necks and not much else. But when you get down toward the south end of town, the freak factor melts away. There's an air force base with humongous planes flying low enough to scalp you, sure, but for the most part it's nice and peaceful.

Rather, it would be nice and peaceful if every summer my mother didn't arrive without a room reservation, just a hundred-count of Aquafina and a beach tote of ancient sunscreens, ready to reset entire circadian rhythms with her monstrous snoring from the pullout.

In fact, this summer, because my nephew, Dax, will be making his first beach appearance—and because nobody wants to miss baby's first boogie-board session—somebody has gone and invited the entire extended family to come to the South Beach Inn. This somebody being one newly anointed Memaw.

"Just think of little booga on that beach," she'd been e-mailing Uncle Jack and Aunt Susan back in Florida for months. They'd previously only been known as *those people;* she'd been giving them the silent treatment for the better part of a decade.

In terrifying old-biddy speak, a *booga* is apparently something that comes out of neither your nose nor your daughter's nose. A *memaw* is somebody who has at least twelve years of Mary Engelbreit desk calendars stashed on a shelf next to the world's largest science experiment concerning nail polish separation (hypothesis: When kept in close contact for ten years or more even chemicals want to get the hell away from each other). Most people would throw away such nonsense when moving across two states, but a true memaw has problems letting go of things, which is why we don't believe her when she says, "It'll be so nice to see Jack and Susie and everyone at the beach."

"So you guys are all talking again?" I ask. "After, what, like eight years?"

"We're perfectly fine," she says, as if nothing bad has ever occurred. She washes beach towels and buys ketchups bigger than pails of pig's blood at Sam's Club in preparation for the trip, singing happy little ditties to Dax the whole time. Her favorite: *If all the raindrops were lemon drops and gumdrops, oh, what a rain that would be.*

Oh, what a world it had already become. Babies change things. When breast-feeding replaces smoking in the house, friends tend to flee. Not even my band, which had been known to empty entire venues of every audience member except for our moms in minutes flat, could clear a room faster than our family. Saints games, birthday parties, cookouts, and festivals, once a gathering of rowdy friends, were now just a showcase for Mom and John's constant bickering and Dax's spit-up, while various cheese dips congealed on the coffee table.

Most people would be lucky to take a vacation whenever they felt this sense of painful, uncontrollable drowning. In my family, you'd be better off drowning yourself to avoid vacation.

Mom and John don't even have enough money to drive to Florida, never mind fly, so they want to carpool, but we are not all down with that idea. My sister has never been trapped in a car with them for ten-plus hours. Only I have ever made that mistake, back in college. Years before Katrina, we'd taken a road trip to see Molly in New Orleans in John's big blue truck. There had been arguing on back roads, nagging over fast food, egregious backseat driving. Then in the dead of night, while I was snoozing, a George Thorogood number had come on the crappy radio station, and they both howled with delight, turning it up and singing along to every word. George Thorogood is like the dog whisperer for certain insane, older white people. He's very soothing to them. For the rest of us, he is the guy known for appropriating Bo Diddley songs in the eighties and putting horrible sax solos in the middle of them.

Even though the thorogood days are over and Mom and John now have diddley, the blue truck still sits on Rampart Street by their apartment. John won't sell it because, quite simply, it's his last vestige of their previous life. He's even told me, "It reminds me of home," so he goes out there and waxes the truck every weekend, and recalls what life was once like with a driveway, hose, and endless ShamWows. My mother does the same thing inside with her ballet slippers and lace-up platform shoes, rubbing the old satin of them, feeling the days of her youth slip beneath her fingers. Entire days and lifetimes can be consumed by this madness if you let it.

Molly and Chris will pay for the gas for Mom and John's trip. They'll take the Focus for better mileage. They'll stop at their house in New Port Richey, to see how it's holding up after Sherry and the man with tattoos on his head abruptly vacated a month before, owing three months' back rent and thousands in water and sewage because of a leaky toilet nobody noticed. They will also pick up Aunt Libby and her dog, Britches, on their way to the beach.

This all leaves me with the worst of options: a ten-hour car ride with a six-month-old baby or a trip to the abandoned House of Hoarder with the added three-hour bonus of a decomposing dog's hot breath. I can't afford a plane ticket. Anyways, I've always been much more of a road tripper for the love of boiled peanuts and Dairy Queen alone.

"Just ride with us," Molly says.

"Maybe," I say, a word I've picked up from my boyfriend of a year. We'll call him Phillip.

He works in film and never makes plans for anything in advance, preferring to revolve his life around Bruce Willis movies that always go directly to DVD. Two days before the vacation though, his movie wraps and for some ungodly reason—guilt, perhaps—he says, "Okay, I guess I can drive us."

❧

The South Beach Inn isn't the Waldorf Astoria. There's no swimming pool or tiki bar or paddleboard lessons. Here you'll find wolf spiders the size of ceiling fans, missing showerheads, mirrored headboards, and what somebody on Yelp recently described as the glorious air of *smokation smokation smokation*! So one can clearly see why Molly enjoys it.

The building itself is easy to miss, camouflaged by sea grapes, tossed on the beach like a log of government cheese somebody flung out a car window on A1A. It's a quiet place when it wants to be, sort of a part-time old folks' home, part-time drug den, which is what all old folks' homes are when you get down to it. Florida is really just the biggest old folks' home of them all.

Every time I bring a new friend here, the reaction is always the same.

"This is the place?" they say.

Phillip says this, inspecting our room. Bottom floor. Mildewy chest of drawers you should never actually put your clothes in. A wall unit as loud as an airboat. The only fancy things are a few complimentary soaps and a large mirror with *Guinness* scrawled across it.

"What's wrong?" I ask him.

"I just pictured it would be different is all."

He lies across the bed and it rolls away from the wall.

"I don't know what you mean," I say.

But I do. I pictured it would all be different too, this vacation, this relationship with him. That we'd be here completely in love, that we'd have a great time. That I could show him off to my family like a new pet, something adorable, something not prone to stray. Instead, we'd lost time taking the scenic route through Pensacola Beach, eaten bad oysters at a bar with a pirate band, and stayed the night at a Holiday Inn outside Tallahassee where Faulknerian Emily hairs haunted the pillows and towels like guitar strings. We'd smoked enough American Spirits to birth a Navajo, navigated enough classic rock stations to know that "Love in an Elevator" is never not playing, eaten our weight in McNuggets, and hardly talked. By the time we hit Paynes Prairie, I had the overwhelming urge to return to New Orleans, crawl into my bed, and sleep with the cat smothering me.

We're coming off a harsh two weeks, after I logged on to

his Facebook page to discover icky private sex messages sent to a woman in France named Veronica. I'd smeared chocolate cake all over his bed in revenge. *I love you and I don't want to lose you,* he told me. *Don't leave me.* So I didn't. We are still together, still figuring things out, but there is the sort of feeling that the good days are behind us, that we've been tainted.

My Hawaiian shirt has faded, I notice, the buttons hanging on by only a few threads. Phillip lies back on the bed. He thinks it's going to be a nice quiet vacation, one full of rest and relaxation. He is wrong.

There's a knock at the door, and it's Aunt Libby, come to see us in her freshly done hair and sky-blue capris. BluBlocker sunglasses make her look like RoboCop.

"Well how-dee-do," she says. "I saw you all come in, so I thought we'd come down and say hello. Say hi, Britches." She lifts Britches by the harness, rescuing him from a dangerous sea of terrazzo his gimp legs cannot navigate. "You must be Phillip. I've heard so much about you."

"Guilty as charged," he jokes.

"Wendy tells me you've been working with Bruce Willis." She knows all about Phillip's work history. Aunt Libby is a very thorough pen pal, crafting twenty-page diatribes that start with wonderful little anecdotes like *I am here to see what's cooking on my left nipple* while waiting in doctors' offices around Holiday, Florida. She practically sends death threats if you don't write back in a timely fashion, even if it's just a simple card with a smiley face and bullet points of every movie star your boyfriend is currently working with.

"I just love those *Die Hard* movies," she says. She's a big movie fan. When we went to see *Titanic* forever ago in the theater, we both left crying, Aunt Libby from heartache and me from the wrenching gas that overtakes my bowels soon after I eat buttered popcorn. Britches likely understands. A constant wave of noxious odor overcomes us and he whimpers. "He's been farting up a storm since we got here. I think he's just excited because we don't travel much, do we, Britches?"

When she does travel though, she makes sure to record every waking moment, which is why she has her laptop up in her room, tucked neatly in a knockoff Vera Bradley case I gave her a few Christmases back. She's ready to present a slide show and PowerPoint concerning her latest bus trip to the Grand Canyon, whenever we're ready to come on by.

"We can do that tomorrow if you like," she says, excusing herself outside because Britches has to poot. "Don't you, Britches? Don't you got to make a big ol' poot?"

Phillip retreats to the bed, but two minutes later there's another knock at the door and he moans. It's Mom and John this time, with Dax trailing them in a baby-mobile, one of those walker-style things on wheels that suspends every baby by severe wedgie and features a plastic table, a veritable Pooh-poo platter, if you will.

"Look who's here, booga," Mom tells Dax. "It's Geegee."

If you're thinking you can sit around for six months imitating some tiny drooler's geegee-gaga language and not have those words thrown back at you in nickname form, you're sorely mistaken. I do a little troll dance that always gets him laughing, and we're having a good time now. Most of us.

There's one long, annoyed sigh from the bedroom. The sound of every relationship I've ever had.

"Memaw is going to put some stuff in Geegee's fridge," Mom tells Dax, who wants out of the walker. Neither she nor John can now speak about themselves without using the third person or addressing Dax in every sentence.

"You want Papa JoJo to lift you out?" John asks. He got the fast-food version of nicknames when *Papa John* stuck. Though now it's been shortened to *Papa JoJo* and also just *JoJo*.

"Where's Phillip, booga?" Mom asks, plucking Dax from John's hands.

"In the bedroom," I say.

"Let's see if there's some room in Geegee's fridge for some things," Mom tells Dax. "Oh, good, there's lots of room for Memaw."

"Yup," I say. *Just wide-open spaces in here.*

"John, go get that cooler."

"I can't carry that by myself, Margie."

"Well, what do you want me to do about it?"

"Maybe Phillip can help," I suggest.

"Um, okay," I hear from the other room.

"Ugh, I can't even tell you what that ride was like with John." Mom wants to bitch the second they're gone. "He missed the turn for Panera Bread, and there's not another exit for about thirty minutes. We had to eat at Quiznos instead."

Phillip and John are back in the door, hauling a cooler with grocery bags of more food piled on top, so Mom can really unload.

"Then Aunt Libby talked the whole ride over from Holiday," she says. "And poor Britches, the old thing can't even take a dump without Aunt Libby talking about it. No, she can't, booga. She can't stop talking."

Dax and I watch while she crams the fridge with extra Bubba Burgers, hot dogs, salad mix, key lime pie, and shrimp. "Did I tell you about how Sherry effin' trashed the place? She did. She effin' trashed the place."

"You want to see the pictures?" John says, getting out his iPhone.

"Maybe later."

But later isn't an option. There are photos of closet doors ripped from their hinges, blades torn off ceiling fans, blinds mangled as if by a disoriented ferret, and strange little symbols crayoned on the walls and doors like satanic messages. Mom hunches inside the fridge, stacking juice boxes, screaming about the things in the garage that the man with tattoos on his head sold for scrap metal.

"Well, you shouldn't have left all that stuff in the first place," Molly says, poking her head in behind Mom's back. "You should've brought everything to New Orleans."

"Oh," Mom says, totally busted. "I thought you were taking a nap."

"Well, I figured I might as well come downstairs to see if you were still talking shit about Sherry like three hours ago."

"Well, she trashed our house."

"Well, she has ovarian cancer, Mom. So you can just stop now."

She does stop. Everybody stops, except Dax, who is back in his Pooh mobile, bashing a button so it restarts *Twinkle, twinkle* every nanosecond. There's Phillip too, who's found a window of solace in the chaos and is now snoring in bed.

"She has cancer?" Mom asks. "That's terrible. When did she find out?"

"She e-mailed me a few days ago. She's going to have surgery."

"Oh. I'm sorry."

"Are you? Are you sorry?"

"How dare you say that."

"Well, all you do is talk shit about her, Mom."

"Jesus," I say. "Can we move this conversation out of my room?"

But nobody listens, they keep picking at each other, so I disappear into the bathroom and return in my swimsuit, heading toward the beach.

"You're going swimming?" Mom calls after me. "We're about to start the grill."

I run toward the water and fling myself in, dunking my head, letting the waves crash over me, letting the undercurrent wash me down the beach until I reach the old Driftwood house that's been here forever. It's a beautiful home built entirely out of wood that washed ashore in another century, I imagine, when ships went down in the awful storms off the coast. Still standing after a hundred years. The type of place I dream of escaping to one day, surrounded by the ocean and howling wind, the peace and quiet. I make fun of my mom all the time for salivating over her home and garden magazines, but here I am doing the same thing in real life, imagining myself trading out a trainwreck for a shipwreck.

❧

Back when I was a kid we didn't really have family reunions. We had something called the Elfers Old-Timers' Picnic, which was about as fun for a kid as the name implies. Elfers is the name of the tiny town that was established before nearby Holiday, and this picnic took place every October, with dozens of descendants of Pasco County's first settlers gathering in places plagued by armies of red ants and horseflies, on top of the usual wet burrito of humidity and swarming mosquitoes. There were always various mayonnaise-based dishes spoiling in the sun for hours, and sand where there should've been no sand. There was always great potato salad and barbecue though, and Mr. Clark's smoked fish, and Uncle David's famous bean soup. Old-timers gathered around folding tables, telling stories while they sweated through their polyester suits. I remember big fat men in Wranglers with suspenders pulled so tight it looked as if they were dressed in a slingshot, as if at any moment a pantsless redneck might cannonball through the sky, over the trees, and into an encroaching suburb's community pool. Sometimes we met at Starkey park, or at the Swartsels' place on Trouble Creek, or even in my grandparents' backyard, but it was always the same drill. The old-timers wilted in the sun, the men in Wranglers tended the grill and barbecue pit, and the little kids got chased around by the bigger kids, kids with sticks and Nerf footballs and ATVs.

When you're no longer a kid, you're expected to participate in the adult activities, like listening to small talk about cysts, high school libraries, taxes, and Republicans, and of course answering queries concerning your own personal life. It's a sad day when the questions relatives want to know are the same ones that often have you crying yourself to sleep: *Where did your boyfriend run off to? What exactly are you doing for work these days? How do you like having your mom in New Orleans?*

It must be the same for my mother, because when asked about the house in New Port Richey, she practically winces. She tries not to talk about Sherry, but she can't help herself. "She had her parents sleeping on a mattress in the living room," Mom tells a second cousin. "And the toilet took to running nonstop for six straight months and left us with an eleven-hundred-dollar water bill."

There are thousands of dollars of repairs to make before they can rent the house again, not to mention the money Sherry managed to screw them out of.

"I can show you all the pictures," John tells everyone. Most people want to talk about their new boats, babies, and barbecue sauce recipes. Mom and John walk around showing off how plagued they are, as if seeking approval for some monstrous canker sore.

It's lunchtime and the sky is beautiful. The grills are being manned by Wranglers and various forms of ugly swim trunks. Down on the sand, there are castles and moats and boogie boards and umbrellas and lots of white pasty relatives and jellyfish, the nice kind that don't sting, dozens of them washed up on the shore. We take over the lawn, drinking our beers and eating things that have been left in the sun. We are forced to squat down and pose in the yard for an album of familial double chins.

"You had your eyes closed in that one," a cousin says every time. "It's a do-over."

All of this and Phillip is still in bed, messing around with his iPhone. He is the opposite of John, never wanting to share any of his search history or photos with you.

"You okay?" he asks when I pop in for a bathroom break.

"Fine," I say. "You?"

"I'm just really tired," he says, stuffing the phone under his pillow and closing his eyes. "I think I may be getting a cold or something."

I open the blinds and he winces. I ask him if he wants to come have some lunch and he doesn't even look up from the pillow, says, "Maybe in a little bit." When I come out of the bathroom, I stare at him cross-eyed while he pokes at his phone.

Finally, he's all, "What? I'm just playing Words with Friends."

When you stop and think about it, Words with Friends really does sound like another name for sexting.

❧

Uncle Jack and his wife, Aunt Susan, arrive, both having lost weight and the urge to scream at the top of their lungs. Mainly they have come under the same spell as Memaw, entranced by their little granddaughters, Lorelie and CiCi. Jack teaches them how to throw horseshoes, lets them chase him around with plastic shovels and bury him in the sand.

"Not like last time I was chased around by a shovel," he says.

Beth, my cousin, has lost weight too, prompting Mom to pull me aside for her pre-told-you-so moment, telling me, "I think she's on the bad shit. Nobody loses weight like that in this family."

It's true. In this family you can stay skinny until the time you hit forty-five. Then the long slow ballooning toward life-size Nerds candy happens from the forehead down. Also, Beth has been working with Susie at my grandmother's book-keeping business, which is not a good sign.

"Is Aunt Susie coming?" I ask.

"Oh, I don't think so," Aunt Libby says. "She's been up in Dixie County since Ricky had his motorcycle accident."

"Ricky has a motorcycle?"

"Son of a bitch *had* a motorcycle," Uncle Jack informs us. "A car ran a red light on Nineteen and ran him right over a month ago. His foot was almost completely severed at the ankle, hanging by a thread, like this here." He lifts up a boogie board by the leash and flops it around for a minute.

"Dear god," I gasp.

"They reattached it, but then the antibiotic drip won't take because ol' Ricky Haunch can't stop drinking."

After lunch, Mom gives free lectures on New Orleans life to anybody who'll listen, but even John falls asleep in the hammock, with a beer leaking down the side of his shirt. Molly's husband, Chris, is passed out under an umbrella at the beach, and Phillip refuses to get out of bed. If we were at the real South Beach, a male slumber party would have a different meaning than this one. But here, at the other South Beach, Mom works her snooze-button siren song, describing her interactions with beggars on Claiborne and her recipe for jambalaya, which she pronounces by combining the *jamba* from *Jamba Juice* with the princess from *Star Wars*.

"Jamba-Leia," she says. "I think I make a pretty good one." She does, for a woman who calls boudin *bow-dan* and says her favorite stage at Jazz Fest is the fais *doo-doo*. But half of the toothless second cousins here don't know anything about it or care. They're just crowding around her because she's the only one who put on bug spray.

"They have a Big Lots *and* a Walmart down in Chalmette," Mom informs them. "That's past the Lower Ninth Ward, which is where we live."

"You live in the Upper Nine," Molly says.

"We do?"

The conversations always circle back to things that have previously been discussed: *Die Hard* movies, Hurricane Katrina, the BP oil spill, the severed foot of Ricky Haunch. The afternoon comes to a close with Aunt Libby's slide-show presentation of her trip to the Grand Canyon.

"So where's that boyfriend?" Aunt Libby asks.

"I don't think he's feeling well," I say. "He may have a cold or something."

"Well that's too bad. I'll make him a plate of food you can take to him when the show is over." Because nothing says *feel better soon* like every form of gelatinous salad to ever sit in the sun.

I'm walking back downstairs when I run into some nut job. We have our nut jobs in this family, but this guy isn't one of them.

He has a folding chair in one hand and a twelve-pack in the other.

"Name is Johnnie Walker," he says. "Don't know if you heard, but party at the fire pit later."

Naturally, when Phillip opens the door in his swimsuit at the stroke of 10:00 P.M., fresh from a day of sleeping, he says he wants to go down to the beach.

"Some creep is having a fire pit," I try to warn him.

"Don't be a loser," he says, two beers into his liquid meal.

There's an extension cord plugged into an outlet on the side of the motel, so we follow it down to the beach, to where Johnnie Walker sits in the light of his bonfire, fiddling with a boom box.

"Lookit who it is, everybody," he says.

Everybody looks it, but nobody knows who it is, or wants to, and the feeling is mutual. The fire is raging, and the locals who've come over have brought along two garbage cans full of chemical-treated two-by-fours and enough weed to ensure nobody will be leaving here with eyebrows or brain cells.

"Damn it," he says, teetering on the verge of some freak-out over the bad reception on his boom box, his Delilah radio show crackling. "I'm going to fix this shit for good. I'll be right back."

He walks back to the motel and returns a few minutes later with a power drill, a box of drill bits, and what looks like a handful of car antennas. In the romantic light of the fire, Johnnie Walker then removes a piece of chemical-treated wood from the garbage can and drills into it six times. He sticks the antennas out of the top like a torture device. The he props it against the boom box. Suddenly, the static disappears, and song after song from the late eighties rings out clear into the cloudless night. The stars above us shine, and the small waves lap on the shore across the sand. No wind, just a beautiful night marred by the sound track to *Top Gun*.

"Come on, beautiful," Johnnie Walker tells one of the ladies who have come down from the streets, the type of middle-aged bottle blonde who would otherwise be barnacled to a beach bar about now. She gets up and dances and so does her friend, both of them tragic in a way that most older strippers are, with small tank tops that look stolen from their children's laundry and lower-belly tattoos that trickle down into the scary place beneath their cutoffs. Phillip watches them for a bit. Sips his beer. Pulls out his phone.

When I first read those French Veronica messages, I called all my girlfriends for advice. My sister said, "Who cares, do what you want—if you love him, just stay with him." Everyone else said to leave him.

"Whoa, whore," my friend who calls everyone *whore* told me. "You need to slow down. Just slow it down and think about what you really want out of this relationship."

But all I could think about was how my life had already slowed down to the point of going nowhere. I was unemployed. My band had destroyed my hearing and voice box. I had my mother showing up at my apartment with jackets, sweaters, old toys, track ribbons, and band uniforms for me to sort through. I'd lost friends out of lack of interest alone, preferring to stay home and leaf through old *Surfer* magazines in my sweatpants. What I wanted out of the relationship was an escape from all that. I wanted the dinners, the wrap parties, the binge drinking, and the sex. It didn't make me feel good, but it made me feel something. So I looked past what Phillip had first barked out when I caught him cyber cheating: *It's a longtime flirtation. I wouldn't expect you to understand,* and *I can't unfriend her on Facebook. We're too good of friends.* I held on. I stayed. I gave him a second chance because the thought of moving on by myself was too painful and scary.

The thing is, there are certain people in this world whom you can give everything to. You can give them a beach, a mountain range, a night so clear you can make out Jupiter, a love so intense it's obsessive, and they'd still rather mess with their cell phone. Ditch these people at the first rest stop.

In the morning, there is the fresh scent of campfire filling up our room, and the feeling that Phillip is not waking up any time soon. It's the last day my extended family will be be visiting, and he doesn't even care if he meets them. I'm outside lathering on the sunscreen with Molly when Johnnie Walker rounds the corner.

"There's my favorite twins," he says. He's never even laid eyes on us together before. "So, I just want to let you know something. I'm being kicked out of this shithole, and I think you all should pack up and leave too."

Some problem with the fire pit and not washing down the deck last night. I can't even process what's going on, he's rambling so fast. "I'm going down to stay at a place that's nicer and they're giving me the same rate," he says. "And they have a hot tub and a Jacuzzi, so if you want to come down there, just let me know."

We head to the beach, where Chris is still sleeping under the umbrella and Dax is eating sand.

"Do you think this is sea lice?" my mother says, pointing to the tiniest red dot her foot has ever seen.

"No," Molly says, glaring at her. Junior year of high school she came home from a band trip to Key West with sea lice so bad she looked like Eric Stoltz in *Mask*. She ran a hundred-plus fever, bathed in oatmeal for four days straight, and is still sensitive about such things.

"I better go take some Benadryl," Mom says. "Come on, booga."

It's all just a ploy to kidnap Dax and show him off as family files in for our last day of reunion. Soon the beach and yard are packed. There are second cousins and their kids who've come over for the day. John has cornered Jim to talk about the Buccaneers. Uncle Jack and the shovel kids are back again, and Aunt Libby watches everyone from the balcony, not having gone near a swimsuit in close to thirty years.

We've eaten lunch and posed for more photos when Phillip emerges from the hotel room and walks into the glaring sun.

"So you're the coon-ass Wendy's dating?" Jack barks at him.

"I guess," he says.

"You want a hot dog?" Libby asks.

"How's your stomach?" Mom asks. "John, go get that Pepto."

Phillip eats a wiener and does his best coon-ass, telling

stories of the bayou, of his dad who hunts deer with a cross-bow. He's very charming when he wants to be, but he doesn't want to be for long. Soon enough he's back in the room, wal-lowing in bed. By evening the wind has picked up, and the family is thinning out, when Johnnie Walker shows up to the hotel.

"You can't keep me from coming to get my shit," Johnnie Walker yells at the manager, who has come out of the office with her cordless phone.

He runs up to the second floor and flings the door of unit thirteen open. It isn't even locked. He starts throwing things over the balcony—surf magazines, a tennis racket, a Sex Wax shirt. Cops are called. There is a sort of lame standoff for an hour until another cop shows up and finally Johnnie Walker removes his belongings and moves them to his van. Some sort of paperwork is being done in the office. A police report.

Johnnie Walker gets ready to drive off into the sunset. He gets in his van and slams the door. He adjusts his sunglasses and turns the keys in the ignition, only to find an empty growl. He does it again, and this time we're all staring. We know all about it. We're not surprised one bit when the van won't start.

He sits in the passenger seat for a few minutes just staring straight ahead, not a single emotion to be read on his face. The cops come out and escort him into the office, and then he re-turns and sits in his van again. Soon enough a tow truck ar-rives, and he waves from the passenger window.

"See you nice folks later," he says.

And maybe we are nice folks, reasonable folks. We've had

our scuffles in the past, but this weekend we are all family. All of us with our double chins and broken capillaries. I've actually gone to a dermatologist about the capillaries on my neck and the guy laughed. "I can't really do anything about those without laser surgery. That's why they call your type a redneck."

In all the photos we look alike, blotchy, red, our foreheads greasy and shining in the sun. If you search through these photos, you won't find a single one of Phillip though. There's no evidence that he was ever even there.

That's a lie. I did take a single photo, after the sun set and everyone went home. Phillip finally woke up, and we went down to the pier for drinks. I snapped his photo while we had mai tais at the bar that sways over the surf, rocking as the tide comes in. We checked out a band called Panama, as bad as their name. Their lead singer wore a Gold's Gym tank top and played the upright bongos during a version of "Iko Iko," the spotlight reflecting off his gold chains and blinding us. We drove over to Heidi's, a German jazz club, to catch the octogenarian nightlife scene and eat salmon canapés as elegant as canned tuna on Ritz crackers. There, a lady named Rhona, vacationing from Jersey, was called onstage to sing with a pianist known for his fifty-year-long cruise-ship tenure.

"This one is for the lovers," she said, looking at us. "There's nothing quite like young love."

We kissed for the old folks, and they clapped and whistled. *We are in love,* my rum-soaked cerebral cortex told my frontal lobes. *We are doing this.* Rhona's voice was one cigarette away from an electrolarynx and her pitch convulsed to the floor like a feather somebody keeps trying to throw across the room.

She had on a zebra-print blouse and mall-walking capris, but she still killed it. *You're the cream in my cawf-fee,* she sang. *You're the salt in my stew. You will always be my necessity, I'd be lost without you.*

Then we were back in the car, howling with laughter, the salt residue thick on the glass, slick on our skin. We flew down the highway lined with sea grape and plumeria, the scent of night-blooming jasmine all around us. I thought, *We could be happy forever.*

The picture I took of him that night was a total throwaway. I didn't use a flash, so it's too dark to tell if he ever did look happy or not, and anyways, the eye is more naturally drawn to the expanse of darkness behind him, out where the pier meets the ocean, and all you see is the moment I could have pushed him off but didn't.

The True Story of One Little Pig

I t's possible I'd been living under a curse when it came to love, ten years' bad luck for breaking up with my first serious boyfriend via e-mail in college. By the time I reached New Orleans a dive-bar palm reader had already pulled me aside from the Megatouch gaming machine and informed me I wouldn't be finding love for a long time. Those were her very words: *True love for you? Not for long time.* She told me she'd been the disco queen of Taiwan thirty years earlier, so you know she'd seen some real tragedies in her day. *Turdy year ago,* she'd said, and waltzed off toward the pathetic light trickling in through the safety plastic and out onto Decatur Street, where she leaned up against two marines who were nearing blackout drunk, all of them vanishing into the night.

I'm not one to advocate the powers of most dive-bar palm readers, but after you find yourself alone on the couch most weekends of your adult life, sewing the seams the cat has clawed open with your cross-stitch supplies and sprawling out half dead with a sweaty bottle of chardonnay on the floor beside you, it can all start to feel rather preordained.

Still, I was clinging to the belief that what Phillip and I had was true love. Sure, he was short and covered in moles, with a strange little distended belly from his Crohn's disease, and the owner of some two dozen fedoras and a pair of purple skinny jeans. But he was nice, funny, and confident, and he had a great job, which is a real pot of gold in this town. Plus, he was helping me out during a tough time.

It was fall. The week Phillip had to leave to work on a film in Anchorage, Alaska. The terms and conditions were this: I got to live rent-free in exchange for dog-sitting, while he got to go light the frozen expanses of the last frontier, primarily Nicolas Cage's and John Cusack's enormous foreheads. As one might expect, it would take many months to capture that type of beauty.

If I'd been put in front of a *Cheaters* background, perched on a leather Office Depot stool to tell all, I might disclose to you how good things had seemed. How Phillip took me to a hot dog party at his grandma's house before he left. How his mom kept buying me all sorts of frighteningly tight clothes from the Dillard's clearance rack that she thought might look good on me, and how Phillip and I had fallen in love over the past year, fishing in his canoe and crafting names for imaginary hybrid animals such as the squirbit and the velocilobster. I might tell you how I'd come to put pressure on the relationship by being broke and hardly employed, backed up two months on bills and student loans with a landlord who kept raising my rent. What I would've been too ashamed to tell you is this: Even if you're so poor you find yourself at a CVS buying a Sprite and a box of tampons with a debit card, and the obese cashier looks deep into your soul and says, "It ain't gone through," and you reswipe the card and she sighs, "It say you got two dollars and seventy-two cents available," never move into your boyfriend's house if you suspect he's a cheater.

It's not so much that I suspected he was cheating as I flat-out knew. I'd already caught him flirting with a former flame on Facebook, which is basically the lowliest form of cheating when you get right down to it: cyber cheating. He never would update his status to say *In a relationship with* me, his girlfriend, *Gwendolyn Knapp.*

"I just don't agree with putting labels on this," he told me whenever I bothered him about our status, and the more jabbing, "It's Facebook, not real life. You know I love you."

But once a guy tells some Veronica in France, *I want to take you out in my canoe and make sweet love to you*—the canoe you yourself drove him to pick up at Academy Sports, the canoe where you spent many sunsets casting for bass on the bayou, only to catch the gnarled nutria nests along the shore, along with your boyfriend's dirty looks—there's really nothing stopping them but a plane ticket and the talent required to not flip a canoe while having sex in it.

My girlfriends knew all about it, giving me a collective eye-roll upon hearing that I'd put most of my possessions in storage and moved out of my apartment uptown.

"You're insane," they said. I'd been told such things before, but in a loving way, the way that says it's okay to shave off half your hair, dye it brown, and rock a bow tie like a female Pee-wee Herman for months on end if it truly makes you happy. But they could see what I could not: that moving in with a guy who wouldn't give up French Veronica and made you feel bad for asking him to is never going to make you happy.

So I moved in.

Phillip's home was basically a large toolshed that his mother had tried to spruce up with paint and oversized satin drapes in the myriad shades of beer shits and horned dung beetles. She was a hairdresser who did interior design and Catholic charity work on the side, which explains everything she was doing in her son's home.

"You like the curtains?" she'd asked when she brought them over after Phillip first bought the house.

"Yeah," I lied.

"Do they look a little wrinkled to you though?"

"Oh, yeah, maybe." Not until she set up an ironing board and forced me to steam them for two hours did I realize I should've kept lying.

I tried to spruce up the house in my own way after moving in, but there's not a lot you can do with power tools too heavy to lift, a six-year-old futon stained to a Pollock, and a hundred-pound television that makes a high-pitched ringing noise after it's been on for more than two minutes. Phillip had kept around two couches that belonged to the previous, very dead owner, and when I brought the cat over to sharpen her claws on the seams, the lights shorted out in the hallway, a sure sign the entity did not approve.

Since I had no idea it's possible to smother somebody from nearly four thousand miles away, I rearranged furniture and brought over my three guitars and two amps, roughly two dozen ceramic squirrels, a few lamps, and a greasy kitchen boom box so I could listen to NPR while cooking my budget pasta. I consolidated his shirts into one drawer to make room for my sweatpants. Brought in my comforter, stuffed his in the closet. I took down the gaudy navy-and-gold-striped shower curtain his mom had hung and put up one that better represented me at thirty years of age: a drab gray panel from the bargain bin.

"Perfect," I said, and my cat agreed, bucking on the matching gray rug until little yarn pubes covered the floor.

I filled his small bookcases with my books. Took down his paltry artwork, which primarily consisted of what his latest ex, Flora, had left him, a charcoal sketch of her boobs she'd had framed at Michael's. This Flora still texted him *because we're still friends* and because she was a costumer who liked to gossip about the film industry, and who had seen us out numerous times without saying hello.

I put her tits facedown in the back bedroom, next to a couple toolboxes, a pressure washer, and a table saw, where the mice liked to crap. They liked to crap in other places too. The whole house was sprinkled with various forms of animal feces, from Kirby's litter box to the land mine of dog doo in the backyard, manned by the small red rat killer, Baccio, and the big Lab, Forty, who kept gnawing at a hot spot on his hind leg until it glistened like a cherry Jolly Rancher in the sun.

❦

There is a fancy, incredibly inviting part of Bayou St. John, but this was not it. The house was more toward the train tracks and interstate, where people who stole cars continually drove them into the water after stripping them of any value. Sometimes the city hauled them up if they were looking for missing persons, and they'd rot on the shore overnight like swamp monsters, all barnacle and algae, shells of their former selves.

Out here, on the edge of ugliness and darkness, the coyotes ran the bayou, packs of them, like mangy wolves in the night. They lived in a place that didn't belong to them and never would, a feeling I knew too well, in an abandoned school up the bayou a ways. I'd sit on the deck with my laptop, opening Facebook to see another new girl, another longtime flirtation, another *miss you so bad xoxo,* and looking up, be startled to find them bolting from under the streetlights on the big Wisner bridge, hauling ass, impervious to my suffering. I'd heard about these coyotes killing small animals, cats and nutria, but I only ever saw them running, ragged but beautiful in the very late night, running for no reason other than a predestined desire to do so.

I took to running myself, covering miles of City Park in the morning, running past wild watermelons and tomatoes on the abandoned golf range, past the fishing holes fecundated with duckweed, until I was wiry, feral, almost deranged.

To say that this was an incredibly low point in my existence would be an understatement, but I tried to keep my spirits up. Mom and Dax would come over on Wednesdays, the day the art museum in City Park was free.

"How is Phillip doing?" she'd ask, taking in a lone Warhol or an African codpiece.

"Oh, he's having a great time," I'd say. "He went to a knife store that also sells piranhas." As if I knew what Alaska was like, as if I knew even half of it.

Occasionally he sent me pictures of himself in his ugliest sweater. Almost every man in America has a version of this sweater, a ribbed Calvin Klein atrocity that zips into a turtleneck. Ugly sweater visits cliff-side brew house. Ugly sweater visits the piranha tank.

Aw, how special, I'd still tell myself. Then he would post the same picture to Facebook, thus depleting it of any thoughtfulness. Thus welcoming a barrage of French Veronicas and California Christies who encouraged his ugly-sweater wearing. *So sexy, baby, when are you coming to visit?*

"Yes, baby, when are you coming to visit?" I badgered him on the phone in my best French accent.

"Are you finished?" he'd say. "I didn't respond to her, you know."

Not publicly anyways, but he did turn right around and tell some Alabama Pam in a pleather corset, *Your tits look amazing. I wish I was Donald.* Donald, naturally, being her husband and all.

"Why did you comment on that Pam lady's boobs like that?"

"Don't you have something better to do than policing me on Facebook? Like work?"

🐷

Of course I didn't. I was working as an instructor in a non-profit after-school arts program for inner-city kids three hours a day. The rest of the day I spent dreading those three hours, and the forty-minute drive it took to get to the school in the run-down burbs across the river on the West Bank. You see, I had always wanted to help make a difference in the world, in New Orleans especially. Myriad studies have shown that kids who can't read by the time they're in third grade are more likely to be incarcerated by the time they hit adulthood. I'd wanted to teach literacy skills and writing to kids, but this meant not being able to live above the poverty line and having no creative freedom due to a prescribed syllabus. I'd been assigned a curriculum from the beginning instead of getting to make my own. The curriculum was based on having students create tableaux, as in creating motionless scenes taken from *The True Story of the Three Little Pigs*. This is a book that teaches children it's okay to eat your asshole neighbors if you accidentally murder them first. Besides all the ravenous homicide and pork belly consumption, the tableaux were about as exciting as they sound: I was asking kids to stand still for more than two seconds at a time.

"It's the way you present it that makes it fun," my curriculum adviser had instructed me from the get-go, straightening an invisible bow like Alexander T. Wolf before sagging toward the floor like a deflated soufflé. "If you present tableau as boring, it will be boring."

If you present yourself as an after-school arts instructor,

you will be an after-school arts instructor. That's why my truck stopped working about a month into the fall semester, just like the first and second band instructors' cars had stopped working, and the modern dance instructor's, and finally the art teacher's van too.

It just so happened that Phillip's Kia Soul, a vehicle as wretched as it sounds, was sitting unused in the driveway and had enough seats to shuttle an entire staff of sad, underpaid after-school arts instructors to the West Bank five days a week.

I guess you can use it, ugly sweater texted from a mountain-top chalet.

Soon I was whizzing around with far better gas mileage than my truck and the worst kinds of body odors, dancer's and musician's, nestling comfortably in the seat cushions.

"Have you gotten your truck fixed yet?" Phillip asked for weeks.

"I only have about a hundred dollars in my bank account," I said. I had made an extra $20 after my band played a gig in a bar where the microphone electrocuted me every time the smoke eater clicked on, but I'd already spent it on gas station Shiraz and a tub of fried chicken, which I ate alone dressed as Jeff Foxworthy on Halloween.

"Are you planning to get the truck fixed any time soon?" he asked.

"I certainly hope so," I said, applying Neosporin to where the spirit gum and handlebar mustache had burned my upper lip. "But shit's not looking too hot right now, Phillip."

My truck lay dead as a slain tauntaun in the front yard for two whole months, months I spent jazzing up my curriculum until the children believed they were attending a workshop in Vogueing. By the time winter break was rolling around, I had little pigs throwing shade at that big bad wolf, houses of straw falling to the floor spread-eagled when I yelled *girl down*.

But each evening, after I got in the Kia Soul and drove the forty minutes back to the bayou, passing the tollbooth that charged $1 every trip, dispensing broke instructors onto the street like New Orleans–flavored Pez, and refilling the tank at $4 a gallon, I felt like the pathetic fang-toothed loser I truly was, alone, broke, and playing Angry Birds in an extra-large Boudreaux's Butt Paste shirt on some dead lady's couch. Then, logging on to Facebook to discover one Tamia was staying with Veronica for a week, and how great would it be if they could have a big Skype date with Phillip, I'd remember the disco queen of Taiwan swaying to Bowie under the disco ball at Aunt Tiki's, whispering, *Not for long time, not for long time*.

Everyone try this fun tableau at home: Late at night, a woman smokes a cigarette on the front deck of another crappy boyfriend's house, staring out into the darkness, past the water, past the train tracks and the cars on the 610, out to where there is nothing but coyotes and oblivion, nothing but the tall grass and the overwhelming feeling that everything is about to fall apart.

You can move into somebody else's house of straw or build your own, but either way, that shit is going to eventually fall apart or go up in flames. I'm not sure when it was that Phillip went totally despondent. He stopped telling me he loved me, stopped texting little pick-me-ups like *G'night, squirbs* and *I want to kiss you so bad*. Often he called when he was on a street somewhere, about to go to a bar with his best boy or some key grips, or he said things like, "Sorry I couldn't answer. I was having dinner with Vanessa Hudgens and her makeup artist."

"Wow, really?"

"Yeah, she's a real sweetheart. How are the boys?"

He'd stopped asking about me altogether. *The boys* were his dogs, as if one might lock their own children in a backyard and never let them come inside. Forty's hot spot was getting bigger, infected, the dog unable to enjoy a day without his hind leg shaking violently. Finally Phillip agreed to let me take him to the vet. He set it up from Alaska, so I wouldn't have to pay. Once we got to the vet, Forty growled and lunged at a male nurse.

"He's being territorial," I was told. "So we'd like you to leave the room."

Then minutes later, they told me, "We need you to come back and put a muzzle on him." I was attempting to tighten the muzzle when the vet then walked toward us, and Forty ripped right out of it, snapping down on her right hand, puncturing it. They gave him meds and encouraged me to get him on Prozac.

"Your dog can't come back unless he's sedated first," they told me.

On the way out he also peed on a basket of chew toys. It was very traumatic for both of us.

"Well he's never done that when I've brought him," Phillip said.

That was around the time he unfriended me on Facebook.

After that, there wasn't much to talk about on the phone besides the mouse problem or the fact that something large and
stank had moved into the attic, alive in the night, so my cat
stayed a stone gargoyle at the edge of the bed.

Our lives were completely different. I cleaned up doo-doo,
watched *Dance Moms*, read Patti Smith's *Just Kids*, played my
guitar on the front deck. He watched a moose get loose on set
and trash thousands of dollars of lighting equipment, and
went out at night, watching the young women in Anchorage
walk around in subzero weather in no more than skintight
dresses and heels.

One night there was a loud explosion and the power went
out, then there were voices on the bayou. I was terrified and
confused. It was 2:00 A.M. and I called Phillip to no answer. I
looked out the front window and saw nothing there, just darkness and beyond it the still water and the gaping expanse of
City Park. Some drunk girl had crashed her car into a phone
pole in front of the house, but I didn't know that because I was
still in a dream state and she'd already moved the car, snuck it
into the dental school parking lot next door, and after I got a
flashlight in one hand and my phone in the other, I saw them
running off, a pair of nightclubbers in skintight dresses, hobbling on their heels from the parking lot to the back of somebody's car stopped on the curb. Then they were gone.

During Christmas break, when Phillip came home, a person named Lalla kept texting and calling from Los Angeles, and he played it off as production meetings and news.

I'd put up a sad little Christmas tree, strung up Christmas lights, hung stockings, baked cookies, but I still felt unwelcome. This was his house. It wasn't my house, and it would never be *our* house. I'd planned to be moved into my own place by now, but I was still completely broke, even after taking on holiday shifts at the cheese shop and picking up more writing gigs, and I could see Phillip was peeved about it all, distant. He didn't want to have sex or snuggle. He was tired, very tired. He wanted to sleep.

"It's okay," he said, cuddling with me. "You can stay for as long as you need to."

On Christmas he sat at my sister's house and yawned while Dax opened his presents, while I opened a box to discover a gray-and-red rabbit stole he got in Anchorage for me, and another box with a beautiful necklace. He yawned at his dad's house during gumbo and potato salad, and then it was onward to his mom and granny's for more yawning.

"I love that fur," his mom said. "Phillip got you that?"

If you look up *cheating* online, one of the signs is expensive and compulsive gift giving. When he flew back out to work another two weeks, I rarely talked to him at all. On the evening before he was set to fly home, I was cleaning up the house when I swept a condom wrapper from under the bed.

WTF? I texted.

Mice? he replied.

I'd been out drinking and watching the Saints game with some friends, who all agreed the evidence was bad. I'd come home and waited for him to walk in the door. My plan was to throw the cat at his face, or a box of live mice, but all the animals had sensed my wrath and hidden in inaccessible places.

"I honestly don't know where it's from," Phillip said as I threw the condom wrapper at his face. "I haven't even been home in the past few months, like, unsupervised."

"Unsupervised?"

"I've had friends stay here too."

"One friend," I said. A nerdy guy in psychology school who hadn't gotten the memo that it's okay for Metallica fans to have short hair now. "You can do better than that."

But he couldn't. Not even as I used my purse as a medieval flail, aiming toward his skull. I broke down crying in the kitchen with the dogs, who'd finally been let in because it was twenty degrees out.

"Why can't you just tell the truth? Why can't you, fucker?"

"I'm sorry, squirbit," he said. "I'm really sorry."

"I'm not your squirbit," I said.

He slid down a wall and then we were both seated, our backs to each other.

I asked all the dumb questions everyone does—Who was she? How could you? When did you? Why? Why? Why?—and he answered. *With Flora. Because we were drunk. Almost a year ago, when I first moved in.* I asked, don't you love me? *Of course I do.* I asked, why did you do it? *I don't know. Because we had good sex. Because it felt good. Because I wanted to.* Nobody ever asks the right questions in this situation. Nobody ever asks themselves, why am I sitting here still talking to this asshole?

Things get skewed when there's heartache and guilt involved. Even the most experienced cheater victims of all time, country music recording artists, go about it all wrong. Dolly Parton begs Jolene not to take her man just because she can, and Loretta Lynn takes the deranged moral high ground with the whole *You ain't woman enough to take my man* (i.e., "Bitch, keep trying") approach. Derangement here is key, as the only way to describe what happens after you find out you've been cheated on is, for lack of a better term, temporary insanity.

Which is probably why, at 3:00 A.M. and shattered, I gave up, went to bed. Phillip got in bed too and spooned me. I didn't even fight it. Four hours later, I stole his phone from the bedside table while he slept, locking myself in the bathroom and gathering more evidence, texts and nudie photos sent by various women. Total derangement. None of it made me feel better. None of it was necessary for any form of healing. I didn't need to see any of it, probably would've been better off not seeing any of it. Still, I got my fill, and left for my sister's house.

Cheating, cyber cheating, emotional cheating, and general infidelity topics are all something you can easily research on the Internet, especially when your life has fallen apart and there's nothing better to do while staying on a futon in a bedroom under construction in the Ninth Ward. Like scabies, staph,

IBS, and depression, cheating does have symptoms. It *is* something you can look up on WebMD, which suggests that it is a disease of sorts, a glitch in the programming anyways, or not. It could just be a normal human condition. It's not as common as HPV, but it's still pretty common. It's not that easy to track because cheaters are usually good liars too. Apparently 40 percent of men who cheat actually meet the people they cheat with at work. The California Christies, the Fuck-Buddy Floras, Alabama Pam with the amazing tits, Los Angeles Lalla with the just-one-tit-exposed artistic selfies, and Bridget the ex-"roommate." There had been so, so many women. Enough women to sink a canoe, enough to capsize it.

There are lists and guides and quizzes you can take to identify if you're being cheated on, or if you yourself are a cheater of the emotional, physical, or even technological kind. There are red flags and sure signs that he's a cheater, but most of them are bewildering at best. Like being extremely horny, which sounds pretty much like every guy I've ever known. Or not being horny at all, or enjoying new music, or just acting straight-up weird, or being highly protective of his cell phone, which is probably a no-brainer. The last text I read was one he'd sent to Bridget just two days earlier about one of her friends that he was interested in: *Is she into dudes? Let's get this started. Also, we need to discuss the current situation.*

The current situation is this: I live on a futon in my sister's spare bedroom, with a paisley-printed sheet over the rotten waterlogged wall. Dax, almost two, lives a room over, and in the mornings he opens the door to my room and scares the cat into the closet. He scares the holy hell out of me, standing near my face like a baby zombie, the scariest of all zombies, until I wake up. My sister's back bedroom is twenty feet from a bodega where just last week we heard a man being shot to death, seven bullets to the torso. Of the two teenagers who shot this man, one was an eighteen-year-old girl named Dajonnaise who smiled pleasingly in her mug shot.

After you've managed to destroy your entire life, after things have gone from bad to worse, when you have nowhere else to turn and no reason to live, you have to go back to your own kind, run with your own pack of wolves.

"I could kill that little bastard," my mother has told me numerous times. "I will strangle him if I ever see him again. I'd like to beat his ass."

She is incredibly supportive in a mildly psychotic way.

Mainly she helps by feeding me. I go over to her house every day for lunch to visit her and Dax. She makes us chicken salad, pulled-pork sandwiches, gumbo with potato salad. I don't say anything about her massive amount of junk anymore, but usually she brings it up.

"I can't find anything in here," she tells me. "I hate this place."

Or she asks me to move a piece of furniture from one room to another, which is no easy task. This is more of a hoarder's nest than the house on Missouri Avenue ever was, and it scares me. They want to buy their own place here, but they can't afford it. There's nobody living at the house on Missouri Avenue, and John can barely swing his mortgage payment and rent. They're hurting bad. I'm hurting bad. We're all hurting bad, so we all scream for ice cream instead of admitting any of our problems.

Still, Dax is a good distraction from our nightmarish lives. He is the perfect size to fit through Mom's pathways and nooks. Lose a fork or knife under the dining table and he's your only chance of retrieving it.

"Brain freeze," he says, tensing up after a bite of Neapolitan. He already knows what a brain freeze is.

Mom spreads patterns out on her bed so we can select outfits of the future, things she may or may not ever make. We pick out fabrics. Dax shows off his button collection, magnet collection, shell collection. We go in the backyard and water the plants, dig for worms, blow bubbles. Dax is the worm master. He digs up the worms. Talks to the worms. Tells them he loves them and puts them back. We watch his cartoons and read his books. We do little performances, the skidamarinky dinky dink and the chicken dance. We hoot like owls and howl likes wolves. We stack his blocks, and he knocks them down and throws them.

"Dax, no throwing," Memaw warns him, but he just throws them harder.

Occasionally he relents, taking a break to drink a bottle or eat some Cheerios, watching me amusedly. I may check my phone, to see if I have an e-mail about a potential job, a potential apartment. Everything in the world is full of potential and totally lacking it, all at once. Anyways, I always have to put the phone away or he'll want to mess around on it. I distract him now, back to the rug.

"Dax, let's pick up these blocks," I say, but he doesn't want to. "Watch me stack," I tell him, piling up the blocks. He gets an agitated look on his face.

"Those are mine," he says.

"So I can't play with them?" I ask. He shrugs and drinks his milk, but I know he'll be around to knock them down in a minute. Still, I don't stop. I stack and stack. I can't help it. I keep rebuilding, even if it's just for the sake of watching things fall apart again.

Black-Eyed Susans

By 2012, Aunt Susie had relocated back to Pasco County for good, taking up her spot at my grandmother's former bookkeeping business, which was then being run by my cousin Beth. She introduced Beth to a friend who sold oxycodone and somewhere along the line they began dealing it out of the office. By 2013, Beth had landed in prison for embezzling money from her clients, and Susie had managed to come away unscathed, salvaging a lone payroll gig that supported her.

It wasn't a surprise when Aunt Libby called to tell my mom the news about Susie landing in the ICU with sepsis, blood poisoning. Susie had been shooting oxycodone for at least three years, along with everybody else in Pasco County, or enough people that the county finally started a prescription-drug outreach program back in 2012. It was all just extremely sad, mind-numbing, especially considering Aunt Susie had gone into the ICU on Aunt Libby's birthday. The day before, poor Britches, who no longer had hair and reeked like a freshly removed cast, had jumped on Aunt Libby's recliner, peed on it one final time, and died.

"But I'm happy to be alive and kicking," Aunt Libby told Mom over the phone. "Happy birthday to me."

It was late July, and I'd been busy writing, gobbling up free-lance gigs, tending the plumeria on the front porch of my micro-scopic apartment, and running my five-mile loop at City Park, where the wildflowers had sprouted up along the edge of the road practically overnight. Hundreds of these delicate yellow flowers were everywhere, and people swarmed them for pho-tos, wading out knee-deep in the field. Daisies really, though I'd always preferred their other name, black-eyed Susans.

"Susie is dying," Mom called to tell me. She was already not having a good week. John had just found out he was get-ting laid off at work, and the house in New Port Richey had sat empty with no tenants for months, so they were on the verge of a financial crisis.

"She has sepsis," I said. "That doesn't mean she's dying."

"Look, I don't want you girls giving me a hard time and telling me I'm negative. She's dying and that's that."

"Jesus, Mom."

"And don't you go telling Molly about John losing his job. I don't want to ruin your vacation."

"She's going to ruin our vacation," Molly said when I called her. We were all set to head to the South Beach Inn in two days, and Molly was pregnant again, unable to drink or smoke, which had immediately turned her personality into something horrendous, like Jabba withdrawing from his extraterrestrial spice. After bearing the bad news about John and Susie, I'd been banished to the backseat torture chamber of the three-year-old. Also, she wouldn't allow me to tell Mom she was pregnant. They were more alike than two sides of an Oreo cookie but needed something in the middle to hold them together: me, the festive, sweet part, acting as glue. It was all very tiring.

For three days, Mom called us at the beach with updates about Susie. There was the fact that Ricky Haunch was nowhere to be found, gone off on a shrimping boat the second she was admitted in the ICU. He'd followed her back down to Pasco around 2012 and had since spent his days leeching onto the Sponge Docks dive-bar scene, which primarily consisted of leathery old drunks who couldn't walk out the door without getting arrested or losing an extremity.

For a week, doctors gave Aunt Susie blood transfusions with usually only Uncle Jack at her side, and Aunt Libby occasionally. Jack had shut down the bookkeeping business before his daughter went to prison, back when he realized they were dealing drugs out of it. But in his older years, he had relaxed about how mean he was toward Susie. He'd seen the worst of her addiction but had learned to control his own temper, his blaming. One time in the early nineties, she almost busted in the back sliding glass door trying to get inside his house, screaming at the top of her lungs. When he got up from bed, he found her sprawled across the white cement near their swimming pool, her wrists slit. There had been drunk altercations with Ricky Haunch, fallings-out where Susie and Jack didn't speak for years. But even after Beth had gone to prison, he'd resumed a relationship with Susie, checking in on her. She'd been doing okay. She'd been gardening and working. She'd been surviving, getting by.

"When she opens her eyes," Mom told me on the phone, "Jack says it's just total fear and panic. She can't say a word."

Things were looking dismal, but then Susie received another transfusion and appeared to be better. The nurses were calling my mother every day. Susie was starting to be responsive.

"She spoke today," Mom said. "But she told Jack that she didn't want to live like this anymore. And nobody can find Ricky Haunch. He has the power of attorney, you know. I don't know if I should go down there or what."

Finally, Ricky did make it back in to shore, cajoled by the other shrimpers on the boat. I didn't hear from Mom for a couple of days, then it came. The call from the hospice in Holiday.

"I made it just in time. She just passed away."

A staph infection had been left untreated for so long it had permeated every part of Susie's body, eating away her organs, her fingers, her toes. Some of her extremities had already turned black. If she'd lived, they would've had to amputate her hands and feet because they were no longer alive, no longer a part of the living organism of her body. She'd been conscious of this all along. She hadn't been in a coma. *I don't want to live like this,* she had said. She knew what was happening. She could hear every word when the doctors entered the room and told Jack, "If we stop antibiotics, she'll die in one to two days."

They stopped the antibiotics and she had died in less than a day.

❧

We cut our vacation short and drove across the state. Tore down Highway 56, a route that didn't even exist when I left for college but was now home to a grotesque amount of gated-community sprawl on old ranch land that still smelled of cows and their shit. Meth addicts in pajamas roamed the gas station aisles while we stopped for gas in town. The houses I grew up thinking were for rich people had all gone to hell. We drove past the VFW where one fall my sister passed out during a marching band performance because she locked her knees in the heat during "The Star-Spangled Banner." We drove past our elementary school, so small and ugly now, though it had been new back then.

I watched out the windows and felt nothing. Indifference. More cow pastures had become gated communities. More houses from the sixties had decayed into the special type of ghetto that comes only after ages of suburban sprawl. Then it appeared before us, coming off the bridge on Perrine Ranch Road to the stoplight on Grand Boulevard: the corner where Aunt Ruby's house used to be.

There wasn't even a car lot there anymore. It was just a large drainage ditch, half full of stagnant brown water and a few pieces of trash. It was awful, but I was prepared for it.

"They tore down Ruby's house," Mom had told me a month earlier. "To widen the road."

Farther down the widened road, my great-grandma's house was now a Dollar Store. Next to it sat my grandmother's house, still standing but bare and foreign. The owner had chopped down all the oak trees and plants surrounding it, painted it a gaudy peach color, which shrank it in size and stature. It had always been grandiose, with the main wall of the house covered in decorative jagged rock. Now it looked like somebody had applied too much concealer to a mountain of cystic acne.

Next to Grandma's, Jack's house looked like a jungle, the plants around it overgrown and beautiful. It was fenced off and gated from the neighbors. The same questionable convenience mart was still across the street. A large truck sat idling in the parking lot of a decrepit church behind it, and a handful of older teens in pajamas and socks eyed it disapprovingly from a yard across the street.

Mom and Jack were having the time of their lives in the swimming pool. The patio was all fixed up, and Beth's husband, Jim, had brought over CiCi and Lorelie. Everybody was in the pool, cousins and family friends. There were two huge coolers of beer, food for days. Feta and olives. Greek salad and shrimp.

"Oh, get out the special feta," Jack ordered somebody, and then there was soft goat feta being spooned onto plates for us with fresh baked bread.

One look at the pool, and Dax was in the water with Memaw, riding a shark raft, swinging on a rope. It was a real affair they had going on back there, with a tiki bar and Christmas lights. Aunt Libby snapped pictures, unable to inquire about relationship or fertility status due to the level of the noise coming off the water.

Because it's impossible to ever have a gathering in this family without some sort of craziness, Jim had brought along his new girlfriend, who'd jumped in the pool in her jean shorts and American-flag T-shirt, even though she didn't know how to swim. She shrieked and nearly drowned, she was so drunk. Then she got out and disappeared down the street.

"Gone home," Jim assured everyone, but she showed back up an hour later, playing the old, out-of-tune piano from Aunt Ruby's that Jack had put in his front room–turned–man cave, which also held the many wonders of parties past, in the form of hundreds of old beer cans lined up on the wall.

"Doesn't it look great in here?" Mom said, marveling at her brother's ability to curate his hoard of tchotchkes. My grandfather's old marlin was on the wall in the living room, and all over the table before it, hundreds of photos of Susie were spread out.

"We're working on some photo boards for the memorial," Mom said.

When my grandmother died, Jack didn't really want Ricky Haunch around, but now that Susie had passed, it was Ricky Haunch organizing the memorial. He wasn't there that night though. He was not on that good of terms with the family. Not then, not ever.

"Shit," Jack said. "Just a few weeks ago Susie was in the yard doing some yard work and a giant cyst the size of a softball burst on her arm."

"Jesus," Mom squealed, chomping down on a few grapes. "I'm trying to eat here."

"It wasn't blood that came out of it," he said. "There was this thing inside it. She comes over to the office the next day and says, 'I thought it was a worm.'"

"Was it a worm?" Molly asks.

"No. It was just the core."

Everything essentially does have a core, no matter how messy. And this is what's left of our own: Dax plays dolls and games with his cousins and the adults shoot the shit over food and drinks in Jack's kitchen. This is the way I always envisioned my grandma's funeral should have gone down. The way many holidays and birthdays did go down. Except Susie wasn't here, and everybody was getting along swimmingly.

"Come look at these pictures," Aunt Susan said. She and Susie had been in the same grade in school, younger than Jack, Mom, and Ricky Haunch.

There was Susie on the beach, looking a lot like myself. There was a photo of her during high school homecoming, wearing what most today would consider a totally un-PC Indian headdress, her body just a Pixy Stick underneath a heavy sweater and jeans. I had a picture like this in my own freshman yearbook, me staring off into the distance, captured in time forever searching for something.

The last time I'd ever seen Susie was the day of my grandma's wake. There had been scabs all over her body, scabs for a lifetime, scabs that would one day kill her. She never went to the doctor. Maybe she was scared of getting turned in to the cops. Maybe she was scared of finding out exactly what was wrong with her. Aren't we all?

Exactly before Grandma died, the first time she went to the

hospital for her stroke, and we all gathered there in Tarpon Springs to see her, Aunt Susie had gone to get a beer and Beth was sent along to basically chaperone. They'd ordered a couple beers at a dive near the Sponge Docks and sat down near a window to drink them. Then some human barnacle had looked over the bar as the daylight shone down on Susie and politely asked, "What's wrong with your arms, sweetheart?"

Molly and I didn't go to the memorial service. We both had to be back to work after the weekend was up, so we drove home. We passed Weeki Wachee Springs, which seemed so old and small then, the parking lot still completely cracked and tragic. I had a copy of the *Oxford American* and some writer from up north had written a piece about how much she wanted to be a mermaid, until she basically went to Weeki Wachee and discovered what it's really like for those women. I guess I always knew that. They'd visit my elementary school, sit in chairs, answer questions, and when they left, you'd see the zippers in back. We knew from the start it wasn't a dream job. We'd go to Buccaneer Bay, the accompanying water park, every summer and freeze our asses off diving down toward the bottom. You could hear the mermaid's muffled performances below the surface, cheerful songs far out of swimming distance.

We arrived back in New Orleans. Mom made it home several days later, with her photo boards and some peace of mind. There was still the question of what would happen with Susie's things, her roosters, her plants. But Mom had spent a good deal of time with her brother, and she was happy about that.

This was all in the summer, and now it's fall in New Orleans. Molly has told Mom she's pregnant. She's expecting a girl, a little Ruby Sue. John has already found another job.

"So that bullet's been dodged," Mom says.

But not all the bullets will be. We all know this. One day Sherry calls Molly out of the blue and tells her she now has a brain tumor. The doctors found it while doing a body scan for her ovarian cancer, which has also returned. And Mom has been putting off a colonoscopy for a year—"Because I don't like doctors," she says. "I don't think I need it."

I hang in there. I go for my run in City Park. The black-eyed Susans are still there, a wall of yellow beauties. One evening the light hits them perfectly and there's nobody around, so I cross the street and run along the edge of them. I have my headphones turned up—Jason Molina is singing, *Mama, here comes midnight with the dead moon in its jaws*—and I have the overwhelming urge to stop. I do. I slow down and walk through the middle of the flowers, and lie down in their yellow mass, watching the big pink sky above me, the last of the sun. I stare at things from the ground up, from the very bottom. I lie there for a while, until some unsuspecting couple comes along. I can hear them close by, as they retrieve a phone from the girl's purse and she wades deeper into the flowers, *so pretty*, she's saying, *Should I do hair up or hair down?* The boyfriend says, *I don't know, babe* and tells her to smile. That's when I pop up. I watch as her face curls, horrified at the sight of me there, covered in sweat and grass and dirt, sending shrapnel of yellow petals into the air, like some hideous beast exposed and running back to the wilds it escaped from.

Acknowledgments

Thank you to the following fabulous humans, for making this book possible: The sexiest man alive (not endorsed by *People* magazine), my badass agent and friend, Christopher Rhodes, and "Cowboy Jim" James Fitzgerald, for everything you two have done for me, and for believing that redneck paradise is a place where dreams occasionally do come true. Thank you so much to Charlie Conrad, Gigi Campo, and the entire team at Gotham for taking a chance on me. Casey Maloney and Beth Parker, you two are my rock stars. To the amazing writer, Xhenet Aliu, kindred spirit, funny person, and honky-tonk angel, thank you for reading these chapters when they were draftier than my cold, dead heart, and thank you for the years of slide guitar, baklava, and also for trying to kill me with your so-called all levels spin class. To the invaluable Beth Staples and Ann Glaviano, my trusty readers and two of the wisest ladies I know, thank you for helping me tame the beast. I am forever indebted to you both. Elizabeth Rudge, your unflinching support and impeccable razzle saved me this year. I am so grateful to have a friend like you. Also, this book couldn't have been written without the help of Kirby the Cat, foot warmer extraordinaire and twenty-four-hour diva.

Many thanks and much love to my people: Jack and Susan, Randi, Beth, Aunt Libby, John, Dax and Ruby Sue, Dad and Kathy, Carol Knapp, Munson and the bros, Bryan and Heather Sandala, Cindy, Brad, and the entire Wojnar/Myers clan, the original Green Demons, Todd Voltz, Jason Core, Bill Humphreys, Keith Hajjar, Seale Paterson, Richard and Danielle Sutton, Eric Cusimano, Judson Felder and the Felder/Rudge clan, Raf Taylor, Kevin Moran, Matt Holt, Christine Gladney, Adrienne Fiakas (Chicachew!), Madison Curry, Nicole Schmitt, Michael Patrick Welch, Amy McKinnon, Candy Sue Ellison, Dawn Johnston, Chris Forscha, Melissa Norris, Ashley Scales, Rich Siegel, Dean Rispler, Andre Price, Kelly Haas, and Laura Jarrait.

Thank you to the teachers who encouraged me to keep writing and inspired me for a lifetime: Jan Ledman at Gulf High School, UCF's Terry Ann Thaxton, and the late, great Jeanne Leiby. A very big special thank-you to Robert Anthony Siegel and Virginia Holman at UNCW.

Most important, thank you, thank you, thank you, Mom and Molly. Without you I'd be nothing. I'd know nothing. I'd have nothing. This book is a love letter to you. I went looking for sappy quotes on the Internet to really class up the ending here, but all I found was this dumb thing from Barbara Bush: "To us, family means putting your arms around each other and being there." But we all know the real version is: "To us, family means putting your arms around each other's necks and being there." May I now present you my glorious neck.

About the Author

Gwendolyn Knapp holds an MFA in creative writing from the University of North Carolina Wilmington. Her fiction has appeared in *Crazyhorse* and *Quarterly West*, and her nonfiction has appeared in *The Southeast Review; Hayden's Ferry Review; The Best Creative Nonfiction, Vol. 2;* and Narrative.ly. She also had a notable-essay mention in *The Best American Essays 2013*. Knapp lives in New Orleans, where she is the editor of *Eater New Orleans*.